I0020369

ARDUINO PLAYS WITH DHT11, IR BLASTER, RELAYS, MOSFET AND ULTRASONIC SENSORS

Arduino plays with DHT11, IR Blaster, Relays, MOSFET and Ultrasonic Sensors !!!

CONTENTS

Arduino and GSM Module

ACKNOWLEDGMENTS

The writer might want to recognize the diligent work of the article group in assembling this book. He might likewise want to recognize the diligent work of the Raspberry Pi Foundation and the Arduino bunch for assembling items and networks that help to make the Internet of Things increasingly open to the overall population. Yahoo for the democratization of innovation!

INTRODUCTION

The Internet of Things (IOT) is a perplexing idea comprised of numerous PCs and numerous correspondence ways. Some IOT gadgets are associated with the Internet and some are most certainly not. Some IOT gadgets structure swarms that convey among themselves. Some are intended for a solitary reason, while some are increasingly universally useful PCs. This book is intended to demonstrate to you the IOT from the back to front. By structure IOT gadgets, the per user will comprehend the essential ideas and will almost certainly develop utilizing the rudiments to make his or her very own IOT applications. These included ventures will tell the per user the best way to assemble their very own IOT ventures and to develop the models appeared. The significance of Computer Security in IOT gadgets is additionally talked about and different systems for protecting the IOT from unapproved clients or programmers. The most significant takeaway from this book is in structure the tasks yourself.

1.HOW TO MEASURE DISTANCE BETWEEN TWO ULTRASONIC SENSORS

Ultrasonic sensor (HC-SR04) is ordinarily used to discover the separation of an item from one specific point. It has been genuinely simple to do this with the Arduino and the code is additionally quite straightforward. In any case, in this article we are gonna to have a go at something else with these well known HC-SR04 sensors. We will take a stab at computing the separation between two Ultrasonic sensors that is, we will make one sensor to go about as transmitter and the other sensor to go about as collector. By doing this we can follow the area of one transmitter utilizing numerous ultrasonic collectors this following is called triangulation and can be utilized for programmed docking robots baggage adherents and other comparative application. Finding the separation between two US sensors may sound to be a genuinely basic undertaking yet I confronted few difficulties which are talked about in this task.

The procedure talked about in this article isn't genuinely exact and probably won't be helpful in any genuine frameworks without alterations. During the hour of this documentation I didn't discover anybody getting results as close as mine so I have quite recently shared my perspectives on how I got it to function with the goal that individuals who are attempting this need not re-imagine the wheel.

Materials Required:

  · HCSR04 Module (2Nos)
  · Arduino (2Nos) - Any model

Circuit Diagram:

Despite the fact that we are going to make one US (Ultrasonic) sensor to fill in as transmitter and the different as recipient it is compulsory associate all the four pins of the sensors with the Arduino. For what reason would it be advisable for us to? A greater amount of that will be examined later, yet for the time being the circuit outline will be as per the following

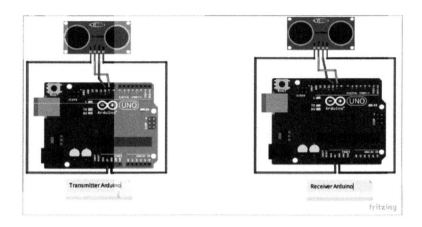

As should be obvious the circuit chart for both Transmitter and recipient are both indistinguishable. Likewise check: Arduino Ultrasonic Sensor Interfacing

How HC-SR04 module actually works:

Before we continue any additionally given us a chance to see how the HC-SR04 sensor functions. The underneath timing Diagram will enable us to comprehend the working.

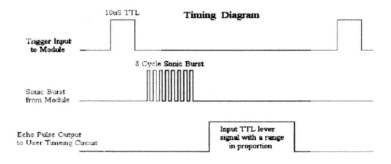

The sensor has two pins Trigger and Echo which is utilized to gauge separation as appeared in the planning outline. First to start estimation we ought to send a Ultrasonic wave from the transmitter, this should be possible by setting the trigger stick high for 10uS. When this is done the transmitter stick will send 8 sonic burst of US waves. This US wave will hit an item ricochet back and will be gotten by the collector.

Here the planning chart demonstrates that once the beneficiary gets the wave it will make the Echo stick go high for a term of time which is equivalent to the time taken for the wave to go from US sensor and reach back to the sensor. This planning chart doesn't appear to be valid.

I secured the Tx (transmitter) some portion of my sensor and checked if the Echo heartbeat got high, and yes it goes high. This implies the Echo heartbeat doesn't sit tight for the US (ultrasonic) wave to be gotten by it. When it transmits the US wave it goes high as well as remains high until the wave returns back. So the right planning outline ought to be something like this demonstrated as follows (Sorry for my poor composition aptitudes)

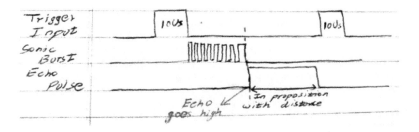

Making your HC-SR04 to work as Transmitter only:

It is practically straight forward to make a HC-SR04 to fill in as transmitter as it were. As appeared in the planning chart you need to pronounce the Trigger stick as yield stick and make it remain high for 10 Microseconds. This will start the Ultrasonic wave burst. So at whatever point we need to transmit the wave we simply need to control the trigger stick of the Transmitter sensor, for which the code is given underneath.

Making your HC-SR04 to work as Receiver only:

As appeared in the planning chart we can't control the ascent of the Echo stick as it is identified with trigger stick. So it is extremely unlikely we could make the HC-SR04 to fill in as recipient as it were. In any case, we can utilize a hack, by simply covering the Transmitter part of the sensor with tape (as appeared in the image underneath) or top the US wave can't escape outside its Transmitter packaging and the Echo stick won't be influenced by this US wave.

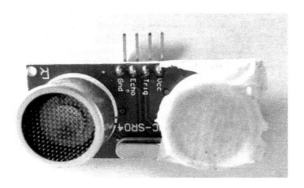

Presently to make the reverberation stick go high we simply need to pull this fake trigger stick high for 10 Microseconds. When this Receiver sensor gets the US wave transmitted by the Transmitter sensor the reverberation stick will go low.

Measuring distance between two Ultrasonic sensors (HC-SR04):

So far we have seen how to make one sensor function as transmitter and the other sensor to fill in as beneficiary. Presently, we need to transmit the ultrasonic wave from transmitter sensor as well as get it with the beneficiary sensor as well as check the time taken for the wave to go from transmitter to collector

sounds simple right?? Be that as it may, unfortu-
nately!, we have an issue here and this won't work.

The Transmitter module as well as Receiver module
are far separated and when the collector module gets
the US wave from the transmitter module it won't
know when the transmitter sent this specific wave.
Without realizing the beginning time we can't ascertain the time taken and therefore the separation. To
take care of this issue the Echo beat of the recipient
module must be made to go high precisely when the
Transmitter module has transmitted the US wave.
At the end of the day, the Transmitter module and
the collector module should trigger simultaneously.
This can be accomplished by the accompanying technique.

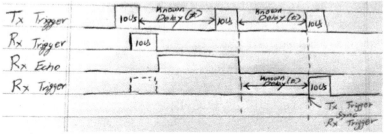

In the above outline, the Tx speaks to Transmitter
sensor and Rx speaks to Receiver sensor. As demonstrated the Transmitter sensor will be made to transmit US waves at an intermittent known postpone-
ment, this is all it needs to do.

In the Receiver sensor we need to some way or another cause the trigger stick to go high precisely during when the transmitter stick goes high. So at first we haphazardly make the Receivers Trigger to go high which will and remain high till the reverberation stick goes low. This reverberation stick will go low just when it gets a US wave from the transmitter. So when it goes low we can accept that the Transmitter sensor just got activated. Presently, with this suspicion when the reverberation goes low we can sit tight for the known deferral and afterward trigger the collectors trigger. This would in part adjust the trigger of both the Transmitter and recipient and consequently you can peruse the quick reverberation beat term utilizing pulseIn() and ascertain the separation.

Program for Transmitter Sensor:

The total program for the transmitter module can be found at the base of the page. It does only trigger the transmitter sensor at an intermittent interim.

```
digitalWrite(trigPin, HIGH);

delayMicroseconds(10);

digitalWrite(trigPin, LOW);
```

To trigger a sensor we need to make the trigger stick to remain high for 10uS. The code to do the equivalent is appeared previously

Program for Receiver Sensor:

In the collector sensor we have spread the Transmitter eye of the sensor to make it sham as talked about before. We can use the previously mentioned procedure to quantify separation between two sensors. The total program is given at the base of this page. Barely any significant lines are clarified underneath

```
Trigger_US();

while (digitalRead(echoPin)==HIGH);

delayMicroseconds (10);

Trigger_US();

duration = pulseIn(echoPin, HIGH);
```

At first we trigger the US sensor by utilizing the capacity Trigger_US() and after that hold up till the reverberation stick remains high utilizing some time circle. When it gets low we sit tight for pre-decided term, this span ought to be somewhere close to 10 to 30 microseconds which can be resolved utilizing experimentation (Or you can utilize ad libbed thought given underneath). After this defer trigger the US again utilizing a similar capacity and afterward utilize the pulseIn() capacity to ascertain the term of the wave.

Presently utilizing a similar old formulae we can ascertain the separation as beneath

distance= duration*0.034;

Working:

Make the associations as clarified in the program. Spread the Tx part of the beneficiary sensor as appeared in the image. At that point transfer the Transmitter code and beneficiary code which are offered beneath to the transmitter and recipient Arduino separately. Open the sequential screen of the recipient module and you should see the separation between two modules being shown.

Note: This strategy is only a belief system and probably won't be exact or fulfilling. Anyway you can attempt the ad libbed thought underneath to show signs of improvement results.

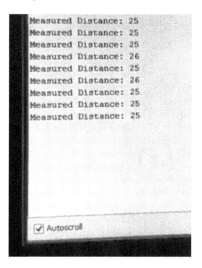

Improvised Idea – calibrating the sensor using a known distance:

The technique that was clarified so far strangely is by all accounts fulfilling, yet it was adequate for my undertaking. Anyway I might likewise want to share the downsides of this technique and an approach to defeat them. One noteworthy disadvantage of this technique is that we expect that the Echo stick of the recipient falls low following the Transmitter sensor has transmitted the US wave which isn't valid since the wave will set aside some effort to make a trip from transmitter to collector. Subsequently the Trigger of the transmitter and the trigger of the collector won't be in impeccable adjust.

To beat this we can align the sensor utilizing a know separation at first. In case the separation is realize we will realize the time taken for the US wave to arrive at the beneficiary from the transmitter. We should keep this time taken as Del(D) as demonstrated as follows.

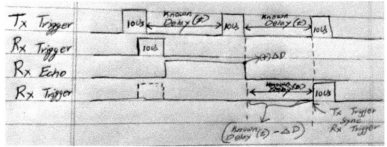

Presently we will precisely know after how much time we should cause the Trigger stick of the Receiver to high to get the opportunity to synchronize with the trigger of the Transmitter. This span can be determined by Known Delay (t) – Del(D). I was not ready to test this thought because of time confinements so I don't know how precise it would function.

Code

Programming code for Receiver part

```
const int trigPin = 9;

const int echoPin = 10;

// defines variables

long duration;
```

```
int distance, Pdistance;

void setup() {

pinMode(trigPin, OUTPUT); // Sets the trigPin as
an Output

pinMode(echoPin, INPUT); // Sets the echoPin as an
Input

Serial.begin(9600); // Starts the serial communica-
tion

}

void loop() {

Pdistance=distance;

Calc();

distance= duration*0.034;

if (Pdistance==distance || Pdistance==distance+1 ||
Pdistance==distance-1 )

{

Serial.print("Measured Distance: ");
```

```
Serial.println(distance/2);

}

//Serial.print("Distance: ");

//Serial.println(distance/2);

delay(500);

}

void Calc()

{

duration=0;

Trigger_US();

while (digitalRead(echoPin)==HIGH);

delay(2);

Trigger_US();

duration = pulseIn(echoPin, HIGH);

}
```

```
void Trigger_US()

{

// Fake trigger the US sensor

digitalWrite(trigPin, HIGH);

delayMicroseconds(10);

digitalWrite(trigPin, LOW);

}
```

Programming code for Transmitter part

```
// defines pins numbers

const int trigPin = 9;

const int echoPin = 10;

// defines variables

long duration;

int distance;

void setup() {
```

```
pinMode(trigPin, OUTPUT); // Sets the trigPin as
an Output

pinMode(echoPin, INPUT); // Sets the echoPin as an
Input

Serial.begin(9600); // Starts the serial communica-
tion

}

void loop() {

// Sets the trigPin on HIGH state for 10 micro sec-
onds

digitalWrite(trigPin, HIGH);

delayMicroseconds(10);

digitalWrite(trigPin, LOW);

delay(2);

}
```

2.INTERFACING NOKIA 5110 GRAPHICAL LCD WITH ARDUINO

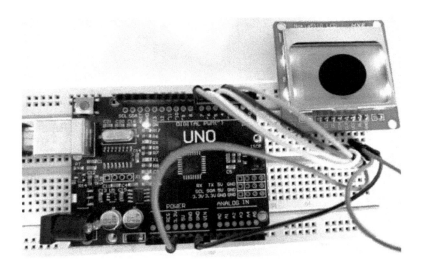

The Iconic name "Nokia 5110" itself ought to have purchased recollections of the strong Nokia cell phone which was famous during the 90's. The model 5110 accompanied a Graphical Display which was adequate enough to go about as a presentation screen for the portable in those days. This screen was equipped for showing everything from alphanumeric characters to little illustrations that is everything required for cell phone. As the earth spun new specialists with glossy touch screens flew in and this showcase are never again being used. Be that as it may, ideally they can be used in gadgets applications where a little designs must be shown and abstain from burning through cash on enormous LCD screens. So in this instructional exercise we will figure out how to interface a Nokia 5110 Graphical LCD with Arduino and make it work.

These LCD have high contrast pixels of measurements 84 × 48. They may look tedious yet at the same time can be utilized to show better than average designs for your tasks and can be effectively utilized with microcontrollers like Arduino. So we should get started....!

Materials Required:

- Arduino Board (any version)
- Nokia 5110 display
- Connecting wires

Nokia 5110 Graphical Display module:

There are two kinds of these Graphical LCDs accessible in the market. One with weld cushions both above and underneath the showcase and the other with patch cushions just on the base of the presentation. The one that we are utilizing have a place with sort 2, where there are cushions just under the presentation. Both the modules work the equivalent and henceforth the associations are the equivalent for both. So independent of what module it is you can pursue the instructional exercise.

As said before Nokia 5110 Graphical LCD has 84 pixels in flat and 48 pixels in vertical. The all out presentation size is 1.72' x 1.72'. The module has 6 information pins utilizing which we can interface it to any microcontroller through SPI correspondence. The interfacing IC that conveys between the presentation and the Arduino is the Philips PCD8544 show controller IC whose datasheet can be found here. In any case in the event that you are utilizing Arduino to speak with this IC, at that point we need not stress over the datasheet since there are libraries that are fit to be downloaded and utilized. The module that we are utilizing here is demonstrated as follows.

Circuit Diagram:

The total circuit outline for associating Nokia5110 Graphical LCD with Arduino is given beneath.

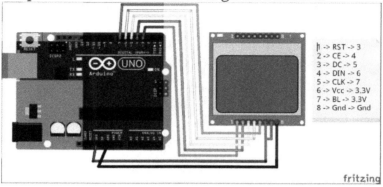

The showcase module has 8 pins which are utilized to set up a SPI correspondence with Arduino. The module is controlled with the 3.3V stick of the Arduino board. Note that these modules chip away at 3.3V rationale and subsequently don't supply 5V to the Vcc stick of the showcases. I have legitimately wired the Pin of presentation to Arduino, in fact the LCD deals with 3.3V rationale and Arduino on 5V rationale on the grounds that at exactly that point I found the LCD to work appropriately. You can utilize a voltage divider to change over 5V to 3.3V whenever required, however for me it works just without the rationale transformation. The associations are truly straightforward and straight forward to make. When you are finished with the associations your set-up would look something like this demonstrated as follows.

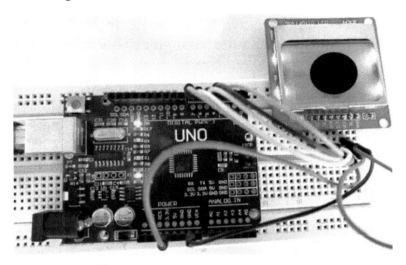

Arduino Program and Working:

Pursue the beneath steps to program your Arduino for the Nokia 5110 Display. The means accept that you have just introduced the Arduino IDE and acquainted with utilizing it.

Stage 1: Open the Arduino IDE on your Computer and select the proper board under apparatuses menu in the wake of interfacing your Arduino to your PC.

Stage 2: Click here to install Nokia 5110 Display Library by Adafruit library from GitHub storehouse.

Stage 3: Once the Zip document is downloaded, select Sketch - > Include Library - > Add .ZIP library and peruse to the area where the ZIP was downloaded.

Note: You will likewise need to download the Adafruit GFX Graphics center which does every one of the circles, content, square shapes, and so on. You can get it from https://github.com/adafruit/Adafruit-GFX-Library and introduce it same way.

Stage 4: Now open the model program by choosing File - > Examples - > Adafruit PCD Nokia 5110 LCD Library - > pcdtest and click on transfer catch

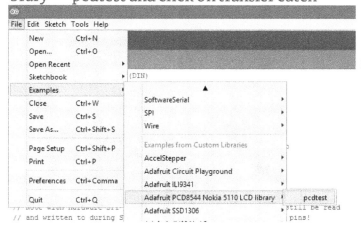

Stage 5: Once the program is transferred, press the reset catch on the Arduino and you should see the model program given toward the finish of this instructional exercise.

You can peruse the model program to comprehend the different inherent capacity that could be utilized to perform different illustrations structure on the LCD. However, let us go above as well as beyond and take a stab at showing Logo on the LCD screen.

Presently open the necessary picture in Paint and resize the picture. The most extreme picture size that we can use for our presentation is 84 × 48.

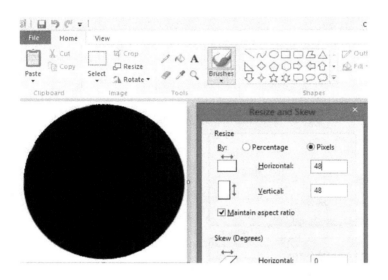

In the case of resizing the picture, spare the picture as bitmap (high contrast) by utilizing the spare as choice in Paint. To show picture as a bitmap on our LCD screen we will require programming that could change over bitmap picture into code. You can download the product by clicking here. Once downloaded unfasten the record and snap on "BitmapEncoder" to dispatch the application. Open the bitmap picture that we simply spared utilizing this product to get the variety of encoded esteems. You can legitimately duplicate these qualities and glue it in your Arduino exhibit. The worth appeared by programming for our logo is demonstrated as follows

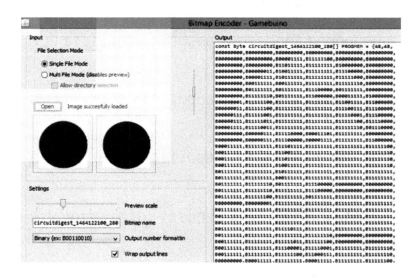

As should be obvious the cluster starts with worth 48, 48 this is the size of our picture. We ought not include this in our cluster. Along these lines, expel the initial two qualities and utilize the rest as the exhibit an incentive in the program. The exhibit will look like underneath. The total program is given toward the finish of this page for your reference.

static const unsigned char PROGMEM Logo[] =

{B00000000,B00000000,B00000000,B00000000,

Anbazhagan K

B00000000,B00000000,

B00000000,B00000000,B00001111,B11111000,B
00000000,B00000000,

B00000000,B00000000,B00001111,B11111111,B
00000000,B00000000,

B00000000,B00000011,B00011111,B11111111,B
11000000,B00000000,

B00000000,B00001110,B00111110,B00111111,B
11110000,B00000000,

B00000000,B00111110,B00111110,B10000000,B
01111100,B00000000,

B00000000,B01111100,B01111100,B11000000,B
00111110,B00000000,

B00000000,B11111100,B01111110,B00000000,B
00001111,B00000000,

B00000001,B11111000,B11111111,B00111111,B
10000111,B10000000,

B00000011,B11111000,B11111111,B11111111,B
11000011,B11000000,

B00000111,B11110001,B11111111,B11111111,B

11100000,B11100000,

B00000111,B11100001,B11111111,B11100011,B
11111000,B01100000,

B00000000,B00000011,B11100000,B00001001,B
11111100,B00000000,

B00000000,B00000111,B11100000,B00011001,B
11111110,B00000000,

B00000000,B00000111,B11000000,B00000001,B
11111111,B10000000,

B00011111,B11111111,B11000111,B11100011,B
11111111,B11111000,

B00111111,B11111111,B10001111,B11111111,B
11111111,B11111100,

B00111111,B11111111,B00011111,B11111111,B
11111111,B11111100,

B00111111,B11111111,B00011111,B11111111,B
11111111,B11111100,

B00111111,B11111110,B00111111,B00111111,B
11111111,B11111110,

B01111111,B11111110,B00111110,B00000000,B

Anbazhagan K

01111111,B11111100,

B01111111,B11111100,B01111100,B11000000,B
00000000,B00000000,

B01111111,B11111100,B01111110,B10000000,B
00000000,B00000000,

B00000000,B00000000,B11111110,B00111111,B
11111111,B11111110,

B00000000,B00000001,B11111111,B11111111,B
11111111,B11111110,

B01111111,B11111111,B11111111,B11111111,B
11111111,B11111110,

B01111111,B11111111,B11111111,B11111111,B
11111111,B11111110,

B01111111,B11111111,B11000111,B11111111,B
11111111,B11111110,

B00111111,B11111111,B10000011,B11111110,B
00000000,B00000000,

B00111111,B11111111,B10110011,B11111000,B
00000000,B00000000,

B00111111,B11111111,B10000001,B11100000,B

00000000,B00000000,

B00111111,B11111111,B11000000,B10000001,B
11111111,B11111100,

B00000000,B00011111,B11111000,B00000111,B
11111111,B11111000,

B00000000,B00000111,B11111110,B00011111,B
11111111,B11111000,

B00000000,B00000001,B11111111,B01111111,B
11111111,B11110000,

B00001111,B11100000,B11111111,B11111111,B
11111111,B11110000,

B00000111,B11111000,B00001111,B11111111,B
11000000,B00000000,

B00000011,B11111100,B00100111,B11111111,B
00000000,B00000000,

B00000011,B11111111,B00110111,B11111100,B
00000000,B00000000,

B00000001,B11111111,B10000111,B11011000,B
00111111,B10000000,

B00000000,B11111111,B11001111,B10000000,B

```
11111111,B00000000,

B00000000,B01111111,B11111111,B10110001,B
11111110,B00000000,

B00000000,B00011111,B11111111,B10110111,B
11111100,B00000000,

B00000000,B00001111,B11111111,B10000111,B
11110000,B00000000,

B00000000,B00000011,B11111111,B11111111,B
11000000,B00000000,

B00000000,B00000000,B11111111,B11111111,B
00000000,B00000000,

B00000000,B00000000,B00001111,B11110000,B
00000000,B00000000,

B00000000,B00000000,B00000000,B00000000,B
00000000,B00000000};
```

Presently to show this bitmap we need to utilize the accompanying lines of code. Where the past information on screen is eradicated and the new bitmap picture is composed.

```
display.clearDisplay();
```

```
display.drawBitmap(20, 0, Logo, 48, 48, 1);

display.display();
```

The line display.drawBitmap(20, 0, Logo, 48, 48, 1); show the position, size and shade of the bitmap picture. The punctuation can be given as.

```
display.drawBitmap    (X_Position,    Y_Position,
Name of Array, length of image, breadth of image);
```

The length and broadness of the picture can be acquired from the initial two component of the cluster separately as told before. At the point when this code is run we will get the bitmap showed on our LCD screen as demonstrated as follows.

You can likewise show straightforward content as demonstrated as follows:

Expectation you comprehended the instructional

exercise and got your Nokia 5110 LCD interfaced with Arduino. With this graphical showcase up in your sleeve you can make numerous activities that require minor designs subtleties.

Code

```
// Nokia5110 display demo program to display logo
//   RST - Pin 3
//   CE  - Pin 4
//   DC  - Pin 5
//   DIN - Pin 6
//   CLK - Pin 7
#include <Nokia5110.h>#include <SPI.h>
#include <Adafruit_GFX.h>
#include <Adafruit_PCD8544.h>
Adafruit_PCD8544 display = Adafruit_PCD8544(7, 6, 5, 4, 3);
/*You can create your own logo by reading the instructions on the tutorial*/


static const unsigned char PROGMEM Logo[] =
{B00000000,B00000000,B00000000,B00000000,B00000000,B00000000,
B00000000,B00000000,B00001111,B11111000,B00000000,B00000000,
B00000000,B00000000,B00001111,B11111111,B00000000,B00000000,
B00000000,B00000011,B00011111,B11111111,B11000000,B00000000,
```

B00000000,B00001110,B00111110,B00111111,B1
1110000,B00000000,
B00000000,B00111110,B00111110,B10000000,B0
1111100,B00000000,
B00000000,B01111100,B01111100,B11000000,B0
0111110,B00000000,
B00000000,B11111100,B01111110,B00000000,B0
0001111,B00000000,
B00000001,B11111000,B11111111,B00111111,B1
0000111,B10000000,
B00000011,B11111000,B11111111,B11111111,B1
1000011,B11000000,
B00000111,B11110001,B11111111,B11111111,B1
1100000,B11100000,
B00000111,B11100001,B11111111,B11100011,B1
1111000,B01100000,
B00000000,B00000011,B11100000,B00001001,B1
1111100,B00000000,
B00000000,B00000111,B11100000,B00011001,B1
1111110,B00000000,
B00000000,B00000111,B11000000,B00000001,B1
1111111,B10000000,
B00011111,B11111111,B11000111,B11100011,B1
1111111,B11111000,
B00111111,B11111111,B10001111,B11111111,B1
1111111,B11111100,
B00111111,B11111111,B00011111,B11111111,B1
1111111,B11111100,
B00111111,B11111111,B00011111,B11111111,B1
1111111,B11111100,

B00111111,B11111110,B00111111,B00111111,B1
1111111,B11111110,
B01111111,B11111110,B00111110,B00000000,B0
1111111,B11111100,
B01111111,B11111100,B01111100,B11000000,B0
0000000,B00000000,
B01111111,B11111100,B01111110,B10000000,B0
0000000,B00000000,
B00000000,B00000000,B11111110,B00111111,B1
1111111,B11111110,
B00000000,B00000001,B11111111,B11111111,B1
1111111,B11111110,
B01111111,B11111111,B11111111,B11111111,B1
1111111,B11111110,
B01111111,B11111111,B11111111,B11111111,B1
1111111,B11111110,
B01111111,B11111111,B11000111,B11111111,B1
1111111,B11111110,
B00111111,B11111111,B10000011,B11111110,B0
0000000,B00000000,
B00111111,B11111111,B10110011,B11111000,B0
0000000,B00000000,
B00111111,B11111111,B10000001,B11100000,B0
0000000,B00000000,
B00111111,B11111111,B11000000,B10000001,B1
1111111,B11111100,
B00000000,B00011111,B11111000,B00000111,B1
1111111,B11111000,
B00000000,B00000111,B11111110,B00011111,B1
1111111,B11111000,

```
B00000000,B00000001,B11111111,B01111111,B1
1111111,B11110000,
B00001111,B11100000,B11111111,B11111111,B1
1111111,B11110000,
B00000111,B11111000,B00001111,B11111111,B1
1000000,B00000000,
B00000011,B11111100,B00100111,B11111111,B0
0000000,B00000000,
B00000011,B11111111,B00110111,B11111100,B0
0000000,B00000000,
B00000001,B11111111,B10000111,B11011000,B0
0111111,B10000000,
B00000000,B11111111,B11001111,B10000000,B1
1111111,B00000000,
B00000000,B01111111,B11111111,B10110001,B1
1111110,B00000000,
B00000000,B00011111,B11111111,B10110111,B1
1111100,B00000000,
B00000000,B00001111,B11111111,B10000111,B1
1110000,B00000000,
B00000000,B00000011,B11111111,B11111111,B1
1000000,B00000000,
B00000000,B00000000,B11111111,B11111111,B0
0000000,B00000000,
B00000000,B00000000,B00001111,B11110000,B0
0000000,B00000000,
B00000000,B00000000,B00000000,B00000000,B0
0000000,B00000000};
void setup()
{
```

```
display.begin();
display.setContrast(50);
display.display(); // show splashscreen
delay(2000);
display.clearDisplay();  // clears the screen and buffer


}
void loop()
{
 display.clearDisplay();
 display.drawBitmap(20, 0,  Logo, 48, 48, 1); // dis-
play.drawBitmap (X_Position, Y_Position, Name of
Array, length of image, breadth of image);
 display.display();
}
```

❖ ❖ ❖

3.CELL PHONE CONTROLLED AC UTILIZING ARDUINO AND BLUETOOTH

In the present current world, any place we go we have bunches of electronic gadgets around us. Yet, out of all, there is just a single gadget that we by and by have in our pockets constantly. Truly, it is our cell phones. Presently Mobile telephones have turned out to be in excess of a gadget utilized for correspondence, they are our cameras, they are our maps, they are our shopping karts and so forth?

With this capacity in our grasp, it is extremely an exhausting plan to utilize Remote controls to control any electronic applications in our home like TV, AC, Home theater and so on. It's continually baffling to go after the AC's Remote from the comfortable solace of our Bed or couch. Subsequently in this undertaking we are going to develop a little set utilizing which you can control the Air conditioner through your Smart telephone utilizing Bluetooth and Arduino. Sounds fascinating right! We should assembled one

Materials Required:

- Arduino Mega 2560
- IR Led
- TSOP (HS0038)
- HC-06
- Any Colour LED as well as 1K Resistor(optional)
- Connecting Wires
- Breadboard

Working Methodology:

All the Remote Controls in our home that we use to control TV, Home Theater, AC and so on work with the assistance of IR Blasters. An IR blaster is only an IR LED which could blaster a sign by dreary beating; this sign will be perused by the collector in the hardware apparatus. For each extraordinary catch on the remote a unique sign will be shot which after perused by the beneficiary is utilized to play out a specific pre-characterized task. In the event that we can peruse this sign turning out from the Remote, we would then be able to copy a similar sign utilizing an IR LED at whatever point required to play out that specific errand. We have recently made an IR Blaster circuit for Universal IR Remote and for Automatic AC Temperature control.

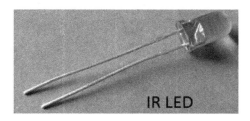

IR LED

A TSOP is an IR Receiver that could be utilized to disentangle the sign originating from the Remotes. We will utilize this TSOP to unravel all the data from our Remote as well as store it on Arduino. At that point utilizing that data and an IR Led we can re-make the IR signals from our Arduino at whatever point required.

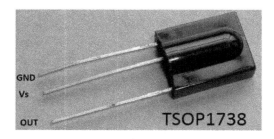

TSOP1738

Pre-requisites:

For this Arduino Bluetooth Controlled AC Project, ensure you have an Arduino Mega as well as no other adaptation of Arduino, since the code size is substantial. Introduce the IR Remote Library utilizing this connect to work with TSOP and IR Blaster.

Working of an AC Remote:

Before we continue into the task take some time as well as notice how your AC remote functions. Air conditioning remotes work in somewhat unique manner contrasted with TV, DVD IR remotes. There may be just 10-12 catches on your Remote, however they will have the option to send a variety of kinds of sign. It means the Remote doesn't send a similar code each time for a similar catch. For instance, when you decline the temperature utilizing the down catch to make it 24°C (degree Celsius) you will get a sign with a lot of information, yet when you press it again to set 25°C you won't get similar information since the temperature is presently 25 and not 24. Likewise the code for 25 will likewise fluctuate for various fan speed, rest settings and so on. So we should not mess with all alternatives and simply concentrate just the temperature esteems with a steady an incentive for different settings.

Another issue is the measure of information that is

being sent for each catch press, ordinary remotes with send either 24 bits or 48 bits however an AC remote may sends up to 228 bits since each sign contains a ton of data like Temp, Fan Speed, Sleep timing, Swing style and so forth. This is the motivation behind why we need an Arduino Mega for better stockpiling alternatives.

Circuit Diagram and Explanation:

Fortunately, the equipment arrangement of this Mobile Phone Controlled Air Conditioner is simple. You can just utilize a breadboard and make the associations as demonstrated as follows.

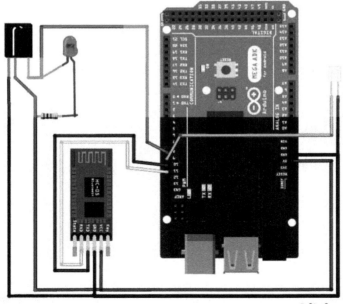

fritzing

The accompanying table can be utilized to confirm your associations.

S.No:	Component Pin	Arduino Pin
1	TSOP – Vcc	5V
2	TSOP – Gnd	Gnd
3	TSOP - Signal	8
4	IR Led – Cathode	Gnd
5	IR Led – Anode	9
6	HC-05 - Vcc	5V
7	HC05 – Gnd	Ground
8	HC05 – Tx	10
9	HC05 – Rx	11

When you associations are done it should look like this demonstrated as follows. I have utilized a Bread-board to clean things, however you can likewise you Male to female wires legitimately to attach all parts

Decoding your AC Remote Signals:

The initial step to control your AC is to utilize TSOP1738 to disentangle AC Remote Control IR Codes. Make every one of the associations as appeared in the circuit chart and ensure you have introduced all the referenced libraries. Presently open the model program "IRrecvDumpV2" can be found at File - > Examples - > IRremote - > IRrecvDumpV2.

```
int recvPin = 8;

IRrecv irrecv(recvPin);
```

Since our TSOP is associate with stick 8, change the

line number 9 to int recPin=8 as appeared previously. At that point Upload the program to your Arduino Mega and open the Serial Monitor.

Point your Remote towards TSOP and press any catch, for each catch you press its separate Signal will be perused by the TSOP1738, decoded by Arduino and showed in the Serial Monitor. For each adjustment in temperature on your Remote you will get an alternate Data. Spare this Data for we will utilize it in our fundamental program. Your sequential screen will look like this, I have additionally demonstrated the Word record on which I have spared the duplicated information.

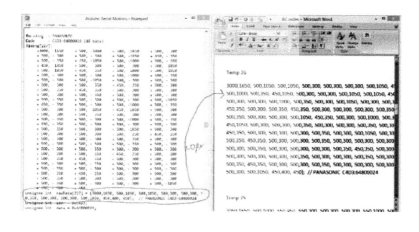

The Screenshot demonstrates the code for setting the temperature at 26°C for my AC remote. In view of your Remote you will get an alternate arrangement of codes. Thus duplicate the codes for all extraordinary degree of temperature. You can check all the AC Remote control IR codes in the Arduino Code given toward the finish of this instructional exercise.

Main Arduino Program:

The total principle Arduino program can be at the base of this page, however you can't utilize a similar program. You need to change the Signal code esteems that we just got from the Ex. sketch. Open the fundamental program on you Arduino IDE and look down to this territory appeared beneath where you need to supplant the cluster esteems with the qualities that you got for your Remote.

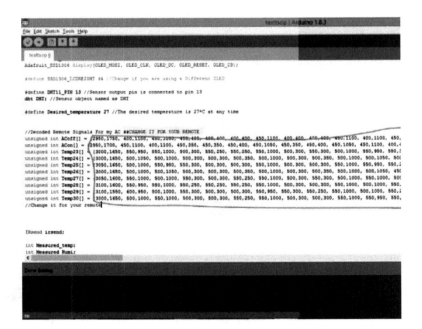

Note that I have utilized 10 Arrays out of which two us used to Turn ON and mood killer the AC while the rest 8 is utilized to set distinctive temperature. For instance Temp23 is utilized to set 23*C on your AC, so utilize the separate code in that Array. When that is done, you simply need to transfer the code to your Arduino.

We have to import two libraries for this task. One is the IRremote library that we just added to Arduino and the other is the in-constructed Software Serial Library that causes us in utilizing the Bluetooth module.

```
#include <IRremote.h> //Lib for IT Blaster and
TSOP

#include <SoftwareSerial.h>// import the serial li-
brary
```

Next we instate the Bluetooth Module on stick 10 and 11 and after that utilization an item called irsend to get to all the IR highlights of the library.

```
SoftwareSerial BT_module(10, 11); // RX, TX

IRsend irsend;
```

Next comes the significant lines of code. This is the place the data to control your AC is available. The one appeared underneath is for my AC remote, you ought to have gotten yours in the past advance.

```
//Decoded Remote Signals For my AC ##CHANGE IT FOR YOUR REMOTE
unsigned int ACoff[] = {2950,1750, 400,1100, 450,1050, 450,400, 400,400, 400,400, 450,1100, 400,400, 400,400,
unsigned int ACon[] = {2950,1700, 450,1100, 400,1100, 450,350, 450,350, 450,400, 450,1050, 450,350, 450,400, ·
unsigned int Temp23[] = {3000,1650, 550,950, 550,1000, 500,300, 550,250, 550,250, 550,1000, 500,300, 550,300,
unsigned int Temp24[] = {3000,1650, 500,1050, 500,1000, 500,300, 500,300, 500,350, 500,1000, 500,300, 500,350,
unsigned int Temp25[] = {3050,1650, 500,1000, 550,950, 550,300, 500,300, 500,300, 550,1000, 500,300, 500,300,
unsigned int Temp26[] = {3000,1650, 500,1000, 500,1050, 500,300, 500,300, 500,350, 500,1000, 500,300, 500,350,
unsigned int Temp27[] = {3050,1600, 550,1000, 500,1000, 550,300, 500,300, 550,250, 550,1000, 500,300, 550,300,
unsigned int Temp28[] = {3100,1600, 550,950, 550,1000, 550,250, 550,250, 550,250, 550,1000, 500,300, 500,300,
unsigned int Temp29[] = {3100,1550, 600,950, 500,1000, 550,300, 500,300, 500,300, 550,950, 550,300, 550,250, !
unsigned int Temp30[] = {3000,1650, 500,1000, 550,1000, 500,300, 500,300, 550,250, 550,1000, 500,300, 500,300,
//Change it for your remote
```

Next inside the void arrangement work, we instate two sequential correspondences. One is Bluetooth at 9600 Baud rate and the other is Serial screen at 57600 baud rate.

```
void setup()

{

    BT_module.begin(9600); //BT works on 9600

    Serial.begin(57600); //Serial Monitor work son 57600

}
```

Inside our void circle (vast circle), we check if there

is anything gotten by the Bluetooth Module. In the event that anything is gotten we store that data in the variable BluetoothData.

```
while (BT_module.available()) //If data is coming

{

    BluetoothData=BT_module.read(); //read it and save it

    Serial.println(BluetoothData); //print it on ser-
ial for testing purpose

}
```

The data gotten by the Bluetooth will be founded on the catch pushed on our Android application that we will introduce in our subsequent stage. When the data is gotten we simply need to trigger the individual IR code like underneath

```
if (BluetoothData == '2')

{

    irsend.sendRaw(Temp23,    sizeof(Temp23)    /
sizeof(Temp23[0]), khz); delay(2000);//Send signal
```

```
to set Temperatue 23C

}
```

Here if the code '2' is gotten we need to set the temperature of the AC to 23°C. Thus we have code from 0 to 9 to play out all the essential control elements of AC. You can allude to the total arduino code toward the finish of this page.

Installing Android Application:

The last advance of the Smart telephone controlled Air Conditioned is to introduce the Android application. The Android application for this venture was made utilizing Processing Android Mode. Handling is a brilliant instrument to make .EXE documents or APK records for you Embedded ventures. It is an Open source stage simply like Arduino and thus totally allowed to download to utilize.

In case you prefer not to get a lot of profound into it, you can just download the APK record from here inside the compress document and introduce it straightforwardly on your cell phone. Open the application and you will get a screen as appeared underneath after which you can continue down to the following stage and appreciate working with the undertaking. Be that as it may, on the off chance that you need to change the program of the application to fit it to your need then you can peruse further.

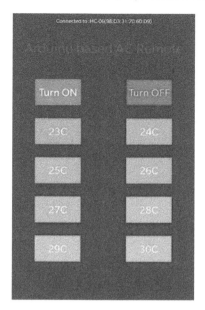

The total program record for Processing code can be downloaded from here. This Zip will have the code and picture source utilizing which the application works. After open the code you can change the accompanying lines to adjust it for your need.

As said before, Processing is like Arduino. So it likewise has a void arrangement and void circle (here draw) capacities. Inside the void arrangement work we will teach the Bluetooth of telephone to associate with Bluetooth of Arduino. My gadget name here is "HC-05" so my line of code will be

```
bt.start(); //start listening for BT connections

bt.getPairedDeviceNames();

bt.connectToDeviceByName("HC-05"); //Connect
to our HC-06 bluetooth module
```

Next inside the load_buttons() capacities you can draw the same number of catches as you need. I have drawn 10 catches as appeared on the Application. Pursued by that we have the read_buttons() work which is utilized to recognize which catch you are contacting. Each catch has a particular shading, so when a client contacts the screen we check which shading he has contacted and figure out which catch he has contacted. An example code to make a catch and select it dependent on shading is demonstrated as follows

```
fill(255,145,3);

rect(width/2-width/4,height/2,
width/4,height/12); fill(255); text("25C",width/2-
width/4,height/2); //button 5

if(color_val==-13589993)
```

```
{byte[] data = {'0'};

bt.broadcast(data);}
```

The line "byte[] information = {'0'};" is a significant line. This is the place we choose which code must be sent to the Arduino through Bluetooth. Here if this catch is squeezed the singe "0" is sent from Bluetooth to Arduino. Likewise we can send an alternate character for various catches. These characters would then be able to be looked at on the Arduino side and separate move can be made.

Feel free to fiddle around the code, on the off chance that you have any questions contact me through the remark area and will give my best in helping you a shot.

Working of Mobile Phone controlled AC:

When you are prepared with your Hardware, Arduino Code and android applications it's a great opportunity to appreciate the yield. Transfer the Arduino Code to your Hardware and spot it confronting your AC. Presently open the android application on your Mobile telephone, if everything is functioning true to form you should see "Associated with: device_name (some code)" as demonstrated as follows

Connected to :HC-06(98:D3:31:70:60:D9)

Presently simply press any catch on your Android application and it should trigger a separate activity on the AC as though you are utilizing a Remote. You can include the same number of catches you need by changing the code and furthermore even computerize your AC dependent on your room temperature or nearness.
Expectation you delighted in the undertaking and comprehended the idea driving it. As consistently in the event that you got any issue in making this work, you can utilize the gatherings to post you questions and get them settled.

APK document for introducing Android Application can be installed from here.

Code
```
/*
 *Bluetooth AC Temperature control using Arduino
and TSOP
 *
S.No: Component Pin Arduino Pin
1 TSOP â€" Vcc  5V
2 TSOP â€" Gnd  Gnd
3 TSOP - Signal  8
4 IR Led â€" Cathode  Gnd
5 IR Led â€" Anode  9
6 HC-05 - Vcc  5V
7 HC05 â€" Gnd  Ground
```

8 HC05 â€" Tx 10

9 HC05 â€" Rx 11

```
*/
#include <IRremote.h> //Lib for IT Blaster and TSOP
#include <SoftwareSerial.h>// import the serial library
SoftwareSerial BT_module(10, 11); // RX, TX
IRsend irsend;
int khz = 38; // 38kHz carrier frequency for the NEC protocol
char BluetoothData; // the data read by Bluetooth Module
int PevData;
//Decoded Remote Signals For my AC ##CHANGE IT FOR YOUR REMOTE
unsigned int ACoff[] = {2950,1750, 400,1100,
450,1050, 450,400, 400,400, 400,400, 450,1100,
400,400, 400,400, 450,1100, 400,1100, 450,350,
450,1100, 400,400, 400,400, 450,1100, 400,1100,
450,400, 400,1100, 400,1100, 450,400, 400,400,
400,1100, 450,350, 450,400, 400,1100, 450,400,
400,400, 400,400, 450,350, 450,350, 450,400,
400,400, 450,350, 450,400, 400,400, 400,400,
450,350, 450,400, 400,400, 400,400, 450,400,
400,400, 400,400, 450,350, 450,350, 450,1100,
400,400, 450,400, 400,1100, 450,1050, 450,400,
400,400, 400,400, 450,350, 450,400, 400,400,
450,350, 450,400, 400,400, 400,1100, 450,350,
450,400, 400,400, 400,400, 450,400, 400,1100,
450,350, 450,400, 400,400, 400,400, 400,1100,
```

450,400, 400,400, 450,350, 450,400, 400,400,
400,400, 450,350, 450,350, 450,400, 400,400,
450,350, 450,400, 400,400, 400,400, 450,350,
450,400, 400,400, 450,350, 450,400, 400,400,
400,400, 450,350, 450,350, 450,400, 450,350,
450,350, 450,400, 450,350, 450,350, 450,350,
450,400, 450,350, 450,350, 450,400, 400,1100,
450,350, 450,350, 450,400, 450,350, 450,350,
450,1100, 450};
unsigned int ACon[] = {2950,1700, 450,1100,
400,1100, 450,350, 450,350, 450,400, 450,1050,
450,350, 450,400, 450,1050, 450,1100, 400,400,
450,1050, 450,350, 450,400, 400,1100, 450,1100,
450,350, 450,1050, 450,1100, 450,350, 450,350,
450,1100, 450,350, 400,400, 450,1100, 450,350,
450,350, 450,400, 400,400, 450,350, 450,350,
450,400, 400,400, 450,350, 450,350, 450,400,
400,400, 450,350, 450,350, 450,400, 450,350,
450,350, 450,1100, 400,400, 450,350, 450,1100,
400,400, 450,350, 450,1100, 400,1100, 450,350,
450,400, 400,400, 450,350, 500,300, 450,400,
450,350, 400,400, 450,1100, 400,400, 450,350,
450,350, 450,400, 400,400, 450,350, 450,1100,
450,350, 400,400, 450,350, 450,400, 450,350,
400,400, 450,400, 450,350, 450,350, 450,350,
450,400, 400,400, 450,350, 450,400, 400,400,
400,400, 400,400, 450,350, 450,400, 450,350,
450,350, 450,400, 450,350, 450,350, 450,350,
450,400, 400,400, 400,400, 450,350, 450,400,
450,350, 400,400, 450,350, 450,400, 450,350,

450,350, 450,350, 450,400, 450,350, 450,1100,
400,400, 400,400, 450,350, 450,350, 450,1100,
400,400,450};
unsigned int Temp23[] = {3000,1650, 550,950,
550,1000, 500,300, 550,250, 550,250, 550,1000,
500,300, 550,300, 500,1000, 550,950, 550,300,
550,950, 550,250, 550,300, 500,1000, 500,1050,
500,300, 500,1000, 550,1000, 500,300, 500,300,
550,1000, 450,350, 500,300, 500,1050, 450,350,
450,350, 450,350, 450,400, 450,350, 450,350,
450,400, 400,400, 450,350, 450,350, 450,350,
450,400, 400,400, 400,400, 450,400, 400,400,
400,400, 450,1100, 400,400, 400,400, 450,1050,
450,400, 400,400, 450,1100, 400,1100, 400,400,
450,350, 450,400, 400,400, 400,400, 450,400,
400,400, 400,400, 450,350, 450,1100, 400,400,
400,400, 450,350, 450,400, 400,400, 450,1100,
400,400, 400,1100, 450,1100, 400,1100, 450,350,
450,400, 400,400, 450,350, 450,350, 450,400,
400,400, 400,400, 450,350, 450,400, 400,400,
450,350, 450,400, 400,400, 400,400, 450,350,
450,400, 400,400, 450,350, 450,350, 450,400,
450,350, 400,400, 450,350, 450,400, 450,350,
450,350, 450,400, 450,350, 450,350, 450,350,
450,400, 400,400, 400,400, 450,350, 450,1100,
400,1100,450,1100,400,1100,450,1100,400,1100,
400,400,450};
unsigned int Temp24[] = {3000,1650, 500,1050,
500,1000, 500,300, 500,300, 500,350, 500,1000,
500,300, 500,350, 500,1000, 500,1050, 500,300,

500,1000, 500,300, 500,350, 500,1000, 500,1050,
500,300, 500,1000, 500,1050, 500,300, 500,300,
500,1050, 500,300, 500,300, 500,1050, 500,300,
500,300, 500,350, 500,300, 500,300, 500,300,
500,350, 500,300, 500,300, 500,300, 500,350,
500,300, 500,300, 500,300, 500,350, 500,300,
500,300, 500,1050, 500,300, 500,300, 500,1050,
500,300, 500,300, 500,1050, 500,1000, 500,300,
500,350, 500,300, 500,300, 500,300, 500,350,
500,1000, 500,1050, 500,1000, 500,300, 500,350,
450,350, 500,300, 500,300, 500,350, 500,1000,
500,300, 500,1050, 500,1000, 500,1050, 500,300,
500,300, 500,350, 500,300, 500,300, 500,300,
500,300, 500,350, 500,300, 450,350, 500,350,
450,350, 450,350, 450,350, 450,400, 400,400,
400,400, 450,400, 400,400, 400,400, 400,400,
450,350, 450,400, 400,400, 450,350, 450,400,
450,350, 450,350, 450,350, 450,400, 450,350,
450,350, 450,350, 500,350, 450,1050, 500,300,
500,1050, 500,1000, 500,1050, 500,1000, 500,1000,
500,350, 550};
unsigned int Temp25[] = {3050,1650, 500,1000,
550,950, 550,300, 500,300, 500,300, 550,1000,
500,300, 500,300, 550,1000, 550,950, 550,250,
550,1000, 500,300, 550,250, 550,1000, 500,1000,
550,300, 550,950, 550,950, 550,300, 500,300,
500,1000, 550,250, 550,300, 550,950, 550,300,
500,300, 500,300, 550,250, 550,300, 500,300,
550,250, 550,250, 600,250, 500,300, 550,250,
550,250, 550,300, 550,250, 500,300, 550,300,

500,300, 500,1000, 550,250, 550,300, 500,1000,
550,250, 550,300, 500,1000, 550,1000, 500,300,
500,300, 550,250, 550,300, 500,300, 500,300,
550,300, 500,1000, 550,950, 550,300, 500,300,
500,300, 550,250, 550,300, 500,300, 550,950,
550,300, 500,1000, 550,1000, 500,1000, 500,300,
550,300, 500,300, 500,300, 550,250, 550,300,
500,300, 500,300, 550,250, 550,300, 500,300,
550,250, 550,250, 550,300, 500,300, 500,300,
550,250, 550,300, 500,300, 550,250, 550,300,
500,300, 500,300, 550,250, 550,250, 550,300,
550,250, 550,250, 550,300, 500,300, 500,300,
550,250, 550,300, 500,300, 500,300, 500,350,
500,1000, 500,1000, 500,1050, 500,1000, 500,1050,
500,300, 550};
unsigned int Temp26[] = {3000,1650, 500,1000,
500,1050, 500,300, 500,300, 500,350, 500,1000,
500,300, 500,350, 500,1000, 500,1050, 450,350,
500,1000, 500,300, 500,350, 500,1000, 500,1050,
500,300, 500,1000, 500,1050, 500,300, 500,300,
500,1050, 500,300, 500,300, 500,1050, 500,300,
500,300, 500,300, 500,350, 500,300, 500,300,
500,350, 500,300, 500,300, 500,300, 500,350,
500,300, 500,300, 500,300, 500,350, 500,300,
500,300, 500,1050, 500,300, 500,300, 500,1050,
450,350, 500,300, 500,1050, 500,1000, 500,300,
500,350, 500,300, 500,300, 500,300, 500,350,
500,1000, 500,300, 500,1050, 500,300, 500,300,
500,300, 500,350, 500,300, 500,300, 500,1050,
500,300, 500,1050, 450,1050, 500,1000, 500,350,

```
500,300,  500,300,  500,350,  450,350,  500,300,
500,300,  500,300,  500,350,  500,300,  500,300,
500,350,  500,300,  500,300,  500,300,  500,350,
450,350,  500,300,  500,350,  450,350,  500,300,
500,300,  500,300,  500,350,  500,300,  500,300,
500,350,  500,300,  500,300,  500,300,  500,350,
500,300,  500,300,  500,350,  450,1050, 500,1000,
500,350,  500,1000, 500,1000, 500,1050, 500,1000,
500,350,500};
unsigned int Temp27[] = {3050,1600, 550,1000,
500,1000, 550,300,  500,300,  550,250,  550,1000,
500,300,  550,300,  500,1000, 550,1000, 500,300,
550,1000, 550,250,  500,300,  550,1000, 500,1050,
500,300,  500,1000, 550,1000, 500,300,  550,250,
550,1000, 550,250,  550,300,  500,1000, 550,300,
500,300,  550,250,  550,300,  500,300,  500,300,
550,300,  500,300,  550,250,  550,300,  500,300,
500,300,  550,300,  500,300,  500,300,  550,300,
500,300,  500,1000, 550,300,  500,300,  550,1000,
500,300,  500,300,  550,1000, 550,1000, 500,300,
500,300,  550,250,  550,300,  500,300,  550,300,
500,300,  500,300,  550,1000, 500,300,  550,250,
550,300,  500,300,  500,300,  500,350,  500,300,
550,250,  550,1000, 500,1000, 550,1000, 500,300,
550,300,  500,300,  550,250,  550,300,  500,300,
500,300,  550,300,  500,300,  500,300,  550,300,
500,300,  550,250,  550,300,  500,300,  500,300,
500,300,  550,300,  550,250,  550,300,  500,300,
500,300,  550,300,  500,300,  500,300,  550,300,
500,300,  500,300,  550,300,  500,300,  500,300,
```

500,300, 500,350, 500,300, 500,350, 500,300, 500,300, 500,1050, 500,1000, 500,1050, 500,1000, 500,350, 500}; // PANASONIC C4D3:64800024
unsigned int Temp28[] = {3100,1600, 550,950, 550,1000, 550,250, 550,250, 550,250, 550,1000, 500,300, 500,300, 550,1000, 500,1000, 550,250, 550,1000, 500,300, 550,250, 550,1000, 550,950, 550,300, 500,1000, 550,950, 550,300, 550,250, 500,1000, 550,300, 500,300, 550,950, 550,300, 500,300, 500,300, 550,250, 550,300, 550,250, 500,300, 550,300, 500,300, 500,300, 550,250, 550,250, 600,250, 500,300, 500,300, 550,300, 500,300, 500,1000, 550,300, 500,300, 500,1000, 550,250, 550,300, 500,1000, 550,1000, 550,250, 550,250, 550,250, 550,300, 500,300, 550,250, 550,1000, 500,1000, 550,250, 550,300, 500,300, 500,300, 550,250, 550,300, 500,300, 550,1000, 500,300, 500,1000, 550,1000, 500,1000, 550,250, 550,300, 500,300, 550,250, 550,250, 550,300, 500,300, 500,300, 550,250, 550,300, 500,300, 550,250, 550,300, 550,250, 500,300, 550,250, 550,250, 550,300, 550,250, 550,250, 550,300, 500,300, 500,300, 550,250, 550,300, 500,300, 550,250, 550,300, 500,300, 500,300, 550,250, 550,250, 550,300, 500,300, 550,1000, 500,300, 500,300, 550,950, 550,1000, 500,1000, 550,1000, 500,300, 550};
unsigned int Temp29[] = {3100,1550, 600,950, 500,1000, 550,300, 500,300, 500,300, 550,950, 550,300, 550,250, 550,1000, 500,1000, 550,250,

```
550,1000,  500,300,  550,250,  550,950,  600,950,
550,250,  550,1000,  500,1000,  550,250,  600,250,
550,950,  550,250,  550,300,  550,950,  550,250,
550,300,  550,250,  550,250,  550,250,  550,300,
550,250,  550,250,  550,300,  500,300,  550,250,
550,250,  550,300,  500,300,  550,250,  550,250,
600,250,  550,950,  550,250,  550,300,  500,1000,
550,250,  550,300,  550,950,  550,1000,  500,300,
500,300,  550,250,  550,250,  550,300,  500,300,
550,250,  550,1000,  500,300,  550,250,  550,300,
500,300,  550,250,  550,250,  550,300,  500,1000,
550,250,  550,1000,  500,1000,  550,1000,  500,300,
500,300,  550,300,  500,300,  500,300,  550,250,
550,250,  550,300,  500,300,  500,300,  550,300,
500,300,  500,300,  550,250,  550,300,  500,300,
500,300,  550,300,  500,300,  500,300,  550,250,
550,250,  550,300,  500,300,  500,300,  550,300,
500,300,  500,300,  550,250,  550,300,  500,300,
500,300,  550,250,  550,300,  500,300,  550,250,
550,250,  550,1000,  500,1000,  550,1000,  500,1000,
550,300, 500};
unsigned  int  Temp30[]  =  {3000,1650,  500,1000,
550,1000,  500,300,  500,300,  550,250,  550,1000,
500,300,  500,300,  550,1000,  550,950,  550,250,
550,1000,  550,250,  550,250,  550,1000,  550,950,
550,300,  500,1000,  550,950,  550,300,  500,300,
550,950,  550,300,  550,250,  550,1000,  500,300,
500,300,  550,250,  550,250,  550,300,  500,300,
550,250,  550,300,  500,300,  500,300,  550,250,
550,300,  500,300,  500,300,  550,300,  500,300,
```

```
500,300,  550,950,  550,300,  500,300,  500,1000,
550,250,  550,300,  550,950,  550,1000,  500,300,
550,250,  550,250,  600,250,  500,300,  550,250,
550,1000,  500,300,  550,250,  550,300,  500,300,
500,300,  550,250,  550,300,  500,300,  550,950,
550,300,  500,1000,  550,950,  550,1000,  500,300,
550,300,  500,300,  500,300,  550,250,  550,300,
500,300,  500,300,  550,250,  550,300,  500,300,
500,300,  550,250,  550,300,  500,300,  500,300,
550,250,  550,300,  500,300,  550,250,  550,300,
500,300,  500,300,  550,250,  550,250,  550,300,
500,300,  550,250,  550,300,  500,300,  500,300,
550,250,  550,300,  500,300,  550,950,  500,1050,
500,1000, 500,350, 500,1000, 500,1000, 500,1050,
500,300, 500};
//Change it for your remote
void setup()
{
 BT_module.begin(9600); //BT works on 9600
   Serial.begin(57600); //Serial Monitor work son
57600
}
void loop()
{
  while (BT_module.available()) //If data is coming
  {
    BluetoothData=BT_module.read(); //read it and
save it
    Serial.println(BluetoothData); //print it on serial
for testing purpose
```

```
}
if(BluetoothData != PevData)
{


   if(BluetoothData == '0')
   {
      irsend.sendRaw(ACon, sizeof(ACon) / sizeof(A-
Con[0]), khz);  delay(2000);//Send signal to Turn On
the AC
   }
   if(BluetoothData == '1')
   {
      irsend.sendRaw(ACoff, sizeof(ACoff) / sizeof(A-
Coff[0]), khz);  delay(2000);//Send signal to Turn on
the AC
   }
   if(BluetoothData == '2')
   {
      irsend.sendRaw(Temp23, sizeof(Temp23) / sizeof(
Temp23[0]), khz);  delay(2000);//Send signal to set
Temperatue 23C
   }
   if(BluetoothData == '3')
   {
      irsend.sendRaw(Temp24, sizeof(Temp24) / sizeof(
Temp24[0]), khz);  delay(2000);//Send signal to set
Temperatue 24C
   }
   if(BluetoothData == '4')
```

```
{
  irsend.sendRaw(Temp25, sizeof(Temp25) / sizeof(
Temp25[0]), khz);   delay(2000);//Send signal to set
Temperatue 25C
}
if(BluetoothData == '5')
{
  irsend.sendRaw(Temp26, sizeof(Temp23) / sizeof(
Temp26[0]), khz);   delay(2000);//Send signal to set
Temperatue 26C
}
if(BluetoothData == '6')
{
  irsend.sendRaw(Temp27, sizeof(Temp27) / sizeof(
Temp27[0]), khz);   delay(2000);//Send signal to set
Temperatue 27C
}
if(BluetoothData == '7')
{
  irsend.sendRaw(Temp28, sizeof(Temp28) / sizeof(
Temp28[0]), khz);   delay(2000);//Send signal to set
Temperatue 28C
}
if(BluetoothData == '8')
{
  irsend.sendRaw(Temp29, sizeof(Temp29) / sizeof(
Temp29[0]), khz);   delay(2000);//Send signal to set
Temperatue 29C
}
if(BluetoothData == '9')
```

```
{
    irsend.sendRaw(Temp30, sizeof(Temp30) / sizeof(
Temp30[0]), khz);    delay(2000);//Send signal to set
Temperatue 30C
}


}
PevData = BluetoothData;
delay(100);// prepare for next data ...
}
```

◆ ◆ ◆

4.INTERFACING HALL EFFECT SENSOR WITH ARDUINO

Sensors have consistently been a crucial segment in any Project. These are the ones which convert the genuine continuous natural information into computerized/variable information with the goal that it very well may be handled by gadgets. There are various sorts of sensors accessible in the market and you can choose one dependent on your prerequisites. In this task we will figure out how to utilize a Hall sensor a.k.a Hall impact sensor with Arduino. This sensor is fit for identifying a magnet and furthermore the post of the magnet.

Why recognize a magnet?, You may inquire. Well there are a ton of uses which for all intents as well as purposes use Hall Effect sensor and we may have never seen them. One basic use of this sensor is to gauge speed in bikes or any pivoting machines. This sensor is additionally utilized in BLDC engines to detect the situation of Rotor Magnets and trigger the Stator curls as needs be. The applications are unending, so how about we figure out how to Interface Hall impact sensor Arduino to include another apparatus in our munititions stockpile. Here are a few undertakings with Hall sensor:

- DIY Speedometer utilizing Arduino as well as Processing Android App

- Computerized Speedometer and Odometer Circuit utilizing PIC Microcontroller

- Computer generated Reality utilizing Arduino as well as Processing

- Attractive Field Strength Measurement utilizing Arduino

In this instructional exercise we will utilize interferes with capacity of Arduino to identify the magnet close to Hall sensor and shine a LED. More often than not Hall sensor will be utilized distinctly with Interrupts as a result of their applications in which high perusing and executing rate is required, subsequently let us likewise use hinders in our instructional exercise.

Materials Required:

- 10k ohm as well as 1K ohm Resistor
- Arduino (Any version)
- Connecting Wires
- LED
- Lobby Effect Sensor (any computerized verison)

Hall Effect Sensors:

Before we plunge into the associations there are not many significant things that you should think about Hall Effect sensors. There are really, two unique sorts of Hall sensors one is Digital Hall sensor and the other is Analog Hall sensor. The advanced Hall sensor can possibly identify if a magnet is available or not (0 or 1) yet a simple corridor sensor's yield fluctuates dependent on the attractive field around the magnet that is it can distinguish how solid or how far the magnet is. In this undertaking will point just at the advanced Hall sensors for they are the most regularly utilized ones.

As the name recommends the Hall Effect sensor works with the guideline of "Lobby impact". As per this law "when a conductor or semiconductor with current streaming one way was acquainted opposite with an attractive field a voltage could be estimated at right points to the present way". Utilizing this method, the corridor sensor will have the option to distinguish the nearness of magnet around it. Enough of hypothesis how about we get into equipment.

Circuit Diagram and Explanation:

The total circuit graph for interfacing Hall sensor with Arduino can be found beneath.

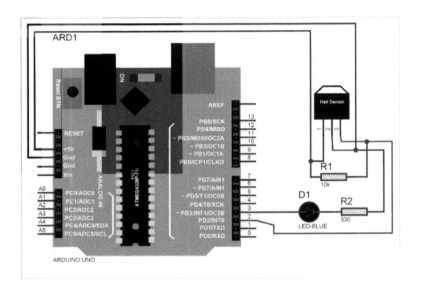

As should be obvious, the corridor impact sensor arduino circuit graph is entirely straightforward. Be that as it may, where we ordinarily commit errors is at making sense of the stick quantities of lobby sensors. Spot the readings confronting you and the principal stick to your left side is the Vcc and after that

Ground and Signal individually.

We are gonna to utilize Interrupts as told before, henceforth the yield stick of Hall sensor is associated with the Pin 2 of the Arduino. The Pin is associated with a LED which will be switched ON when a magnet is recognized. I have essentially made the associations on a breadboard and it looked to some degree like this beneath once finished.

Hall Effect Sensor Arduino Code:

The total Arduino code is only couple of lines and it tends to be found at the base of this page which can be legitimately transferred to your Arduino Board. On the off chance that you have to know how the program functions read further.

We have one information, which is the sensor and one

yield which is a LED. The sensor must be associated as an intrude on info. So inside our arrangement work, we instate these pins and furthermore make the Pin 2 to fill in as an interfere. Here stick 2 is called Hall_sensor and stick 3 is called LED.

```
void setup() {

  pinMode(LED, OUTPUT); //LED is a output pin

  pinMode(Hall_sensor, INPUT_PULLUP); //Hall sensor is input pin

  attachInterrupt(digitalPinToInterrupt(Hall_sensor), toggle, CHANGE); //Pin two is interrupt pin which will call toggle function

}
```

At the point when there is an interfere with identified, the switch capacity will be called as referenced in the above line. There are many intrude on parameters like Toggle, Change, Rise, Fall and so on yet in this instructional exercise we are distinguishing the difference in yield from Hall sensor.

Presently inside the switch work, we utilize a variable called "state" which will simply change its state to 0 if effectively 1 and to 1 if effectively zero. Along these lines we can make the LED turn ON or Turn OFF.

```
void toggle() {

  state = !state;

}
```

At long last inside our circle work, we simply need to control the LED. The variable state will be modified each time a magnet is identified consequently we use it to decide whether the LED should remain on or off.

```
void loop() {

  digitalWrite(LED, state);

}
```

Arduino Hall Effect Sensor Working:

When you are prepared with your Hardware and Code, simply transfer the Code to the Arduino. I have utilized a 9V battery to control the entire set-up you can utilize any ideal power source. Presently bring the magnet near the sensor and your LED will shine and in the event that you remove it will mood killer.

Note: Hall sensor is Pole delicate, which means one side of the sensor can either recognize just North Pole or just South Pole and not both. So in the event that you bring a south post near the north detecting surface your LED won't sparkle.

What really occurs inside is, the point at which we bring the magnet near sensor the sensor changes its state. This change is detected by the intrude on stick which will call the switch work inside which we change the variable "state" from 0 to 1. Thus the LED will turn on. Presently, when we move the magnet away from the sensor, again the yield of sensor will change. This change is again seen by our intrude on proclamation and consequently the variable "state" will be changed from 1 to 0. Along these lines the LED whenever Turned off. Similar rehashes each time you bring a magnet near the sensor.

Expectation you comprehended the task and appreciated structure something new.

Code

```
const byte ledPin = 13;
const byte interruptPin = 2;
volatile byte state = LOW;
int val=0;
void setup(){
pinMode(ledPin, OUTPUT);
pinMode(interruptPin, INPUT_PULLUP);
attachInterrupt(digitalPinToInterrupt(interrupt-
Pin), test, CHANGE);
Serial.begin(9600);
}
void loop(){
digitalWrite(ledPin, state);
Serial.println(val/2);
}
void test(){
state = !state;
val++;
}
```

5.AUTOMATIC AC TEMPERATURE CONTROLLER UTILIZING ARDUINO, DHT11 AND IR BLASTER

An AC (Air Conditioner) which was once viewed as an extravagance thing and was uniquely to be found in enormous inns, motion picture corridors, cafés and so forth... In any case, presently nearly everybody has an AC in our home to prevail over the mid year/winter and the individuals who have it, stress over one normal thing. That is their high power utilization and chargers because of it. In this task we are going to make a little Automatic Temperature Control Circuit that could limit the power chargers by changing the AC temperature naturally dependent on the Rooms temperature. By fluctuating the set temperature occasionally we can abstain from making the AC to work for lower temperature esteems for quite a while and subsequently making it expend less power.

A wide part of us would have encountered a circumstance where we need to change the Air Conditioner's set temperature to various qualities during various occasions of the day, in order to keep us comfortable all through. To robotize this procedure this undertaking utilizes a Temperature sensor (DHT11) which peruses the present temperature of the room and dependent on that worth it will send directions to the AC through an IR blaster like the AC's Remote. The AC will respond to these directions as though it is responding to its Remote and in this way alter the temperature. As your room's temperature changes, the Arduino will likewise alter your AC's set temperature to keep up your temperature in simply the manner in which you need it to be. Sounds cool right?... How about we perceive how to assemble one.

Materials Required:

- TSOP1738 (HS0038)
- Arduino Mega 2560
- DHT11 Temperature/Humidity Sensor
- IR Led
- Breadboard
- Any Colour LED as well as 1K Resistor(optional)
- Connecting Wires

Working Methodology:

All the Remote Controls in our home that we use to control TV, Home Theater, AC and so on work with the assistance of IR Blasters. An IR blaster is only an IR LED which could blaster a sign by dull beating; this sign will be perused by the collector in the gadgets apparatus. For each extraordinary catch on the remote a remarkable sign will be shot which after perused by the beneficiary is utilized to play out a specific pre-characterized task. On the off chance that we can peruse this sign turning out from the Remote, we would then be able to mirror a similar sign utilizing an IR LED at whatever point required to play out that specific errand. We have recently made an IR Blaster circuit for Universal IR Remote.

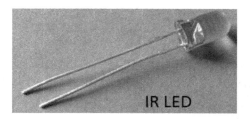

IR LED

A TSOP is an IR Receiver that could be utilized to interpret the sign originating from the Remotes. This Receiver will be interfaced with Arduino to flag for each catch and after that an IR Led will be utilized with Arduino to mirror the sign at whatever point required. Along these lines we can deal with our AC utilizing Arduino.

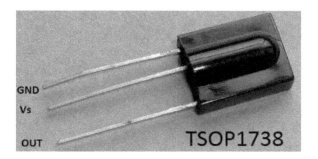

GND
Vs
OUT   TSOP1738

Presently, all that is left is to peruse the Temperature worth utilizing DHT11 and teach the AC in like manner utilizing the IR signals. To make the undertaking look increasingly alluring and easy to use I have likewise included an OLED show that show the present Temperature, Humidity and AC set temperature. Become familiar with utilizing OLED with Arduino.

Pre-requisites:

This Automatic AC Temperature Controller task is marginally best in class for tenderfoot's level, anyway with assistance of couple of different instructional exercises anybody can fabricate this with matter of time. So on the off chance that you are a flat out novice to OLED, DHT11 or TSOP then compassionately fall back to these instructional exercises beneath where you can gain proficiency with the nuts as well as bolts and how to begin with these. The rundown may appear to be bit long, however trust me it's simple and worth adapting, likewise it will open ways to numerous new tasks.

- Fundamental circuit utilizing TSOP and IR LED to under their working

- Fundamental interfacing guide for DHT11 with Arduino

- Essential interfacing guide for OLED with Arduino

- Interfacing TSOP with Arduino to Read IR remote qualities

Ensure you have an Arduino Mega and some other rendition of Arduino, since the code size is substantial. Likewise check in the event that you have just introduced the accompanying Arduino libraries if not introduce them structure the connection beneath

- IR Remote Library for TSOP as well as IR Blaster
- Adafruit Library for OLED
- GFX Graphics Library for OLED
- DHT11 Sensor Library for Temperature sensor

Working of an AC Remote:

Before we continue into the undertaking take some time as well as notice how your AC remote functions. Air conditioning remotes work in somewhat extraordinary manner contrasted with TV, DVD IR remotes. There may be just 10-12 catches on your Remote, however they will have the option to send a variety of kinds of sign. Which means the Remote doesn't send a similar code each time for a similar catch. For instance, when you decline the temperature utilizing the down catch to make it 24°C (degree Celsius) you will get a sign with a lot of information, however when you press it again to set 25°C you won't get similar information since the temperature is currently 25 and not 24. Additionally, the code for 25 will likewise fluctuate for various fan speed, rest settings and so on. So how about we not tinker with all choices and simply concentrate just the temperature esteems with a consistent incentive for different settings.

Another issue is the measure of information that is being sent for each catch press, ordinary remotes with send either 24 bits or 48 bits however an AC remote may sends up to 228 bits since each sign contains a ton of data like Temp, Fan Speed, Sleep timing, Swing style and so forth. This is the motivation behind why we need an Arduino Mega for better stockpiling alternatives.

Circuit Diagram and Explanation:

Fortunately, the equipment arrangement of this Automatic AC Temperature Control Project is simple. You can just utilize a breadboard and make the associations as demonstrated as follows.

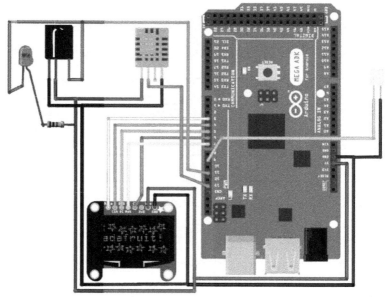

fritzing

The accompanying table can likewise be utilized to check your associations.

S.No:	Component Pin	Arduino Pin
1	OLED – Vcc	5V
2	OLED – Gnd	Gnd
3	OLED- SCK, D0,SCL,CLK	4
4	OLED- SDA, D1,MOSI, Data	3
5	OLED- RES, RST,RESET	7
6	OLED- DC, A0	5

7	OLED- CS, Chip Select	6
8	DHT 11 – Vcc	5V
9	DHT 11 – Gnd	Gnd
10	DHT 11 – Signal	13
11	TSOP – Vcc	5V
12	TSOP – Gnd	Gnd
13	IR Led – Anode	9
14	IR Led – Cathode	Gnd

When you associations are done it should look like this demonstrated as follows. I have utilized a Breadboard to clean things, however you can likewise you Male to female wires straightforwardly to attach all segments

Decoding your AC Remote Signals:

The initial step to control your AC is to utilize TSOP1738 to unravel AC Remote Control IR Codes. Make every one of the associations as appeared in the circuit chart and ensure you have introduced all the referenced libraries. Presently open the model program "IRrecvDumpV2" which can be found at File - > Examples - > IRremote - > IRrecvDumpV2. Transfer the program to your Arduino Mega and open the Serial Monitor.

Point your Remote towards TSOP and press any catch, for each catch you press its separate Signal will be perused by the TSOP1738, decoded by Arduino and showed in the Serial Monitor. For each adjustment in temperature on your Remote you will get an alternate Data. Spare this Data for we will utilize it in our principle program. Your sequential screen will look something like this, I have likewise demonstrated the Word record on which I have spared the duplicated information.

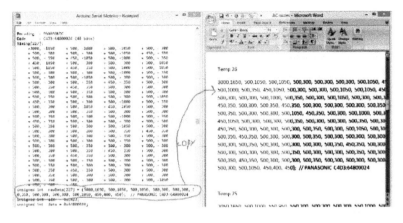

The Screenshot demonstrates the code for setting the temperature at 26°C for my AC remote. In light of your Remote you will get an alternate arrangement of codes. Additionally, duplicate the codes for all unique degree of temperature. You can check every AC Remote control IR codes in the Arduino Code given toward the finish of this instructional exercise.

Main Arduino Program:

The total fundamental Arduino program can be found at the base of this page, however you can't utilize a similar program. You need to change the Signal code esteems that we just got from the Example sketch above. Open the principle program on you Arduino IDE and look down to this territory appeared underneath where you need to supplant the cluster esteems with the qualities that you acquired for your Remote.

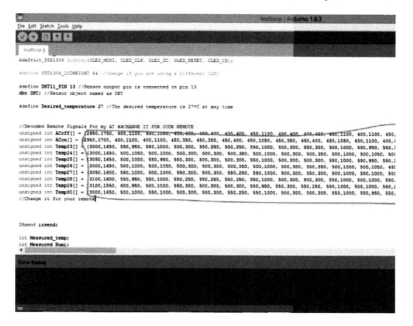

Note that I have utilized 10 Arrays out of which two used to Turn ON and mood killer the AC while the rest 8 is utilized to set diverse temperature. For instance Temp23 is utilized to set 23°C on your AC, so utilize the separate code in that Array. When that is done, you simply need to transfer the code to your Arduino and Place it inverse of you AC and appreciate the Cool Breeze.

The Explanation of the code goes as pursues, first we need to utilize the DHT1 temperature sensor to peruse the Temperature and Humidity and show it on the OLED. This is finished by the accompanying code.

```
DHT.read11(DHT11_PIN); //Read the Temp and
Humidity

Measured_temp = DHT.temperature + temp_er-
ror;

Measured_Humi = DHT.humidity;

// text display tests

display.setTextSize(1);

display.setTextColor(WHITE);

display.setCursor(0,0);

display.print("Temperature:    ");    display.print(
Measured_temp);display.println("C");

display.setCursor(0,10);

display.print("Humidity:  ");  display.print(Meas-
ured_Humi);display.println("%");
```

When we know the Temperature of the room we simply need to contrast it and the ideal worth. This ideal
worth is a consistent worth which is set as 27°C (Degree Celsius) in my program. So dependent on this

correlation we will set a relating AC temperature as demonstrated as follows

```
if (Measured_temp == Desired_temperature+3) //If
AC is ON and measured temp is very high than de-
sired

{

    irsend.sendRaw(Temp24,     sizeof(Temp24)    /
sizeof(Temp24[0]), khz); delay(2000);//Send signal
to set 24*C

  AC_Temp = 24;

}
```

Here the AC will be set to 24°C when the Measured temperature is 30°C (since wanted temp is 27). So also we can make numerous If circles to set diverse degree of temperatures dependent on the deliberate temperature as demonstrated as follows.

```
if (Measured_temp == Desired_temperature-1) //If
AC is ON and measured temp is low than desired
value

{
```

```
  irsend.sendRaw(Temp28,    sizeof(Temp28)    /
sizeof(Temp28[0]), khz); delay(2000);//Send signal
to set 28*C

  AC_Temp = 28;

}

if (Measured_temp == Desired_temperature-2 ) //If
AC is ON and measured temp is very low than de-
sired value

{

  irsend.sendRaw(Temp29,    sizeof(Temp29)    /
sizeof(Temp29[0]), khz); delay(2000);//Send signal
to set 29*C

  AC_Temp = 29;

}

if (Measured_temp == Desired_temperature-3 ) //If
AC is ON and measured temp is very very low de-
sired value

{

  irsend.sendRaw(Temp30,    sizeof(Temp30)    /
sizeof(Temp30[0]), khz); delay(2000);//Send signal
```

to set 30*C

```
  AC_Temp = 30;

}
```

Working of Automatic AC Temperature Control System:

At the point when your Code and equipment is prepared, Upload the Code to your Board and you should view the OLED showing something like this.

Presently place the hardware inverse to your Air Conditioner and you see the AC's temperature getting controlled dependent on the rooms temperature. You can have a go at expanding the temperature close to the DHT11 sensor to check if the AC's temperature is controlled.

You can change the program to play out any ideal activity; all you need is the code that you gotten from the model sketch. Expectation you comprehended this Automatic Temperature Controller undertaking and delighted in structure something fundamentally the same as.

Code

```
/*
 * Automatic AC Temperature control using Arduino
and TSOP

 *
   S.No: Component Pin Arduino Pin
 1 OLED – Vcc  5V
 2 OLED – Gnd  Gnd
 3 OLED- SCK, D0,SCL,CLK 4
 4 OLED- SDA, D1,MOSI, Data  3
 5 OLED- RES, RST,RESET  7
 6 OLED- DC, A0  5
 7 OLED- CS, Chip Select 6
 8 DHT11 – Vcc 5V
 9 DHT11 – Gnd Gnd
 10 DHT11 – Signal  13
 11 TSOP – Vcc  5V
 12 TSOP – Gnd Gnd
```

```
13  IR Led – Anode 9
14  IR Led – Cathode Gnd
*/
```

```
#include <IRremote.h> //Lib for IT Blaster and TSOP
#include <SPI.h> // Inbuilt Lib
#include <Wire.h> //Inbuilt Lib
#include <Adafruit_GFX.h> //Lib for OLED
#include <Adafruit_SSD1306.h> //Lib for OLED
#include <dht.h> //Library for dht11 Temperature
and Humidity sensor (Download from Link in article)
```

```
// Assign pins for OLED (Software config.)
#define OLED_MOSI 3
#define OLED_CLK  4
#define OLED_DC   5
#define OLED_CS   6
#define OLED_RESET 7
Adafruit_SSD1306 display(OLED_MOSI, OLED_CLK,
OLED_DC, OLED_RESET, OLED_CS);
```

```
#define SSD1306_LCDHEIGHT 64 //Change if you are
using a Different OLED
#define DHT11_PIN 13 //Sensor output pin is con-
nected to pin 13
dht DHT; //Sensor object named as DHT
#define Desired_temperature 27 //The desired tem-
perature is 27*C at any time
//Decoded Remote Signals For my AC ##CHANGE IT
```

FOR YOUR REMOTE

```
unsigned  int  ACoff[]  =  {2950,1750,  400,1100,
450,1050, 450,400,  400,400,  400,400,  450,1100,
400,400,  400,400,  450,1100, 400,1100, 450,350,
450,1100, 400,400,  400,400,  450,1100, 400,1100,
450,400,  400,1100, 400,1100, 450,400,  400,400,
400,1100, 450,350,  450,400,  400,1100, 450,400,
400,400,  400,400,  450,350,  450,350,  450,400,
400,400,  450,350,  450,400,  400,400,  400,400,
450,350,  450,400,  400,400,  400,400,  450,400,
400,400,  400,400,  450,350,  450,350,  450,1100,
400,400,  450,400,  400,1100, 450,1050, 450,400,
400,400,  400,400,  450,350,  450,400,  400,400,
450,350,  450,400,  400,400,  400,1100, 450,350,
450,400,  400,400,  400,400,  450,400,  400,1100,
450,350,  450,400,  400,400,  400,400,  400,1100,
450,400,  400,400,  450,350,  450,400,  400,400,
400,400,  450,350,  450,350,  450,400,  400,400,
450,350,  450,400,  400,400,  400,400,  450,350,
450,400,  400,400,  450,350,  450,400,  400,400,
400,400,  450,350,  450,350,  450,400,  450,350,
450,350,  450,400,  450,350,  450,350,  450,350,
450,400,  450,350,  450,350,  450,400,  400,1100,
450,350,  450,350,  450,400,  450,350,  450,350,
450,1100, 450};
unsigned  int  ACon[]  =  {2950,1700,  450,1100,
400,1100, 450,350,  450,350,  450,400,  450,1050,
450,350,  450,400,  450,1050, 450,1100, 400,400,
450,1050, 450,350,  450,400,  400,1100, 450,1100,
450,350,  450,1050, 450,1100, 450,350,  450,350,
```

```
450,1100, 450,350, 400,400, 450,1100, 450,350,
450,350, 450,400, 400,400, 450,350, 450,350,
450,400, 400,400, 450,350, 450,350, 450,400,
400,400, 450,350, 450,350, 450,400, 450,350,
450,350, 450,1100, 400,400, 450,350, 450,1100,
400,400, 450,350, 450,1100, 400,1100, 450,350,
450,400, 400,400, 450,350, 500,300, 450,400,
450,350, 400,400, 450,1100, 400,400, 450,350,
450,350, 450,400, 400,400, 450,350, 450,1100,
450,350, 400,400, 450,350, 450,400, 450,350,
400,400, 450,400, 450,350, 450,350, 450,350,
450,400, 400,400, 450,350, 450,400, 400,400,
400,400, 400,400, 450,350, 450,400, 450,350,
450,350, 450,400, 450,350, 450,350, 450,350,
450,400, 400,400, 400,400, 450,350, 450,400,
450,350, 400,400, 450,350, 450,400, 450,350,
450,350, 450,350, 450,400, 450,350, 450,1100,
400,400, 400,400, 450,350, 450,350, 450,1100,
400,400,450};
unsigned int Temp23[] = {3000,1650, 550,950,
550,1000, 500,300, 550,250, 550,250, 550,1000,
500,300, 550,300, 500,1000, 550,950, 550,300,
550,950, 550,250, 550,300, 500,1000, 500,1050,
500,300, 500,1000, 550,1000, 500,300, 500,300,
550,1000, 450,350, 500,300, 500,1050, 450,350,
450,350, 450,350, 450,400, 450,350, 450,350,
450,400, 400,400, 450,350, 450,350, 450,350,
450,400, 400,400, 400,400, 450,400, 400,400,
400,400, 450,1100, 400,400, 400,400, 450,1050,
450,400, 400,400, 450,1100, 400,1100, 400,400,
```

```
450,350,  450,400,  400,400,  400,400,  450,400,
400,400,  400,400,  450,350,  450,1100, 400,400,
400,400,  450,350,  450,400,  400,400,  450,1100,
400,400,  400,1100, 450,1100, 400,1100, 450,350,
450,400,  400,400,  450,350,  450,350,  450,400,
400,400,  400,400,  450,350,  450,400,  400,400,
450,350,  450,400,  400,400,  400,400,  450,350,
450,400,  400,400,  450,350,  450,350,  450,400,
450,350,  400,400,  450,350,  450,400,  450,350,
450,350,  450,400,  450,350,  450,350,  450,350,
450,400,  400,400,  400,400,  450,350,  450,1100,
400,1100, 450,1100, 400,1100, 450,1100, 400,1100,
400,400, 450};
unsigned int Temp24[] = {3000,1650, 500,1050,
500,1000, 500,300,  500,300,  500,350,  500,1000,
500,300,  500,350,  500,1000, 500,1050, 500,300,
500,1000, 500,300,  500,350,  500,1000, 500,1050,
500,300,  500,1000, 500,1050, 500,300,  500,300,
500,1050, 500,300,  500,300,  500,1050, 500,300,
500,300,  500,350,  500,300,  500,300,  500,300,
500,350,  500,300,  500,300,  500,300,  500,350,
500,300,  500,300,  500,300,  500,350,  500,300,
500,300,  500,1050, 500,300,  500,300,  500,1050,
500,300,  500,300,  500,1050, 500,1000, 500,300,
500,350,  500,300,  500,300,  500,300,  500,350,
500,1000, 500,1050, 500,1000, 500,300,  500,350,
450,350,  500,300,  500,300,  500,350,  500,1000,
500,300,  500,1050, 500,1000, 500,1050, 500,300,
500,300,  500,350,  500,300,  500,300,  500,300,
500,300,  500,350,  500,300,  450,350,  500,350,
```

```
450,350,  450,350,  450,350,  450,400,  400,400,
400,400,  450,400,  400,400,  400,400,  400,400,
450,350,  450,400,  400,400,  450,350,  450,400,
450,350,  450,350,  450,350,  450,400,  450,350,
450,350,  450,350,  500,350,  450,1050,  500,300,
500,1050, 500,1000, 500,1050, 500,1000, 500,1000,
500,350, 550};
unsigned int Temp25[] = {3050,1650,  500,1000,
550,950,  550,300,  500,300,  500,300,  550,1000,
500,300,  500,300,  550,1000,  550,950,  550,250,
550,1000,  500,300,  550,250,  550,1000,  500,1000,
550,300,  550,950,  550,950,  550,300,  500,300,
500,1000,  550,250,  550,300,  550,950,  550,300,
500,300,  500,300,  550,250,  550,300,  500,300,
550,250,  550,250,  600,250,  500,300,  550,250,
550,250,  550,300,  550,250,  500,300,  550,300,
500,300,  500,1000,  550,250,  550,300,  500,1000,
550,250,  550,300,  500,1000,  550,1000,  500,300,
500,300,  550,250,  550,300,  500,300,  500,300,
550,300,  500,1000,  550,950,  550,300,  500,300,
500,300,  550,250,  550,300,  500,300,  550,950,
550,300,  500,1000,  550,1000,  500,1000,  500,300,
550,300,  500,300,  500,300,  550,250,  550,300,
500,300,  500,300,  550,250,  550,300,  500,300,
550,250,  550,250,  550,300,  500,300,  500,300,
550,250,  550,300,  500,300,  550,250,  550,300,
500,300,  500,300,  550,250,  550,250,  550,300,
550,250,  550,250,  550,300,  500,300,  500,300,
550,250,  550,300,  500,300,  500,300,  500,350,
500,1000, 500,1000, 500,1050, 500,1000, 500,1050,
```

103

Anbazhagan K

500,300, 550};
unsigned int Temp26[] = {3000,1650, 500,1000,
500,1050, 500,300, 500,300, 500,350, 500,1000,
500,300, 500,350, 500,1000, 500,1050, 450,350,
500,1000, 500,300, 500,350, 500,1000, 500,1050,
500,300, 500,1000, 500,1050, 500,300, 500,300,
500,1050, 500,300, 500,300, 500,1050, 500,300,
500,300, 500,300, 500,350, 500,300, 500,300,
500,350, 500,300, 500,300, 500,300, 500,350,
500,300, 500,300, 500,300, 500,350, 500,300,
500,300, 500,1050, 500,300, 500,300, 500,1050,
450,350, 500,300, 500,1050, 500,1000, 500,300,
500,350, 500,300, 500,300, 500,300, 500,350,
500,1000, 500,300, 500,1050, 500,300, 500,300,
500,300, 500,350, 500,300, 500,300, 500,1050,
500,300, 500,1050, 450,1050, 500,1000, 500,350,
500,300, 500,300, 500,350, 450,350, 500,300,
500,300, 500,300, 500,350, 500,300, 500,300,
500,350, 500,300, 500,300, 500,300, 500,350,
450,350, 500,300, 500,350, 450,350, 500,300,
500,300, 500,300, 500,350, 500,300, 500,300,
500,350, 500,300, 500,300, 500,300, 500,350,
500,300, 500,300, 500,350, 450,1050, 500,1000,
500,350, 500,1000, 500,1000, 500,1050, 500,1000,
500,350, 500};
unsigned int Temp27[] = {3050,1600, 550,1000,
500,1000, 550,300, 500,300, 550,250, 550,1000,
500,300, 550,300, 500,1000, 550,1000, 500,300,
550,1000, 550,250, 500,300, 550,1000, 500,1050,
500,300, 500,1000, 550,1000, 500,300, 550,250,

550,1000, 550,250, 550,300, 500,1000, 550,300,
500,300, 550,250, 550,300, 500,300, 500,300,
550,300, 500,300, 550,250, 550,300, 500,300,
500,300, 550,300, 500,300, 500,300, 550,300,
500,300, 500,1000, 550,300, 500,300, 550,1000,
500,300, 500,300, 550,1000, 550,1000, 500,300,
500,300, 550,250, 550,300, 500,300, 550,300,
500,300, 500,300, 550,1000, 500,300, 550,250,
550,300, 500,300, 500,300, 500,350, 500,300,
550,250, 550,1000, 500,1000, 550,1000, 500,300,
550,300, 500,300, 550,250, 550,300, 500,300,
500,300, 550,300, 500,300, 500,300, 550,300,
500,300, 550,250, 550,300, 500,300, 500,300,
500,300, 550,300, 550,250, 550,300, 500,300,
500,300, 550,300, 500,300, 500,300, 550,300,
500,300, 500,300, 550,300, 500,300, 500,300,
500,300, 500,350, 500,300, 500,350, 500,300,
500,300, 500,1050, 500,1000, 500,1050, 500,1000,
500,350, 500}; // PANASONIC C4D3:64800024
unsigned int Temp28[] = {3100,1600, 550,950,
550,1000, 550,250, 550,250, 550,250, 550,1000,
500,300, 500,300, 550,1000, 500,1000, 550,250,
550,1000, 500,300, 550,250, 550,1000, 550,950,
550,300, 500,1000, 550,950, 550,300, 550,250,
500,1000, 550,300, 500,300, 550,950, 550,300,
500,300, 500,300, 550,250, 550,300, 550,250,
500,300, 550,300, 500,300, 500,300, 550,250,
550,250, 600,250, 500,300, 500,300, 550,300,
500,300, 500,1000, 550,300, 500,300, 500,1000,
550,250, 550,300, 500,1000, 550,1000, 550,250,

550,250, 550,250, 550,300, 500,300, 550,250,
550,1000 500,1000, 550,250, 550,300, 500,300,
500,300, 550,250, 550,300, 500,300, 550,1000,
500,300, 500,1000, 550,1000, 500,1000, 550,250,
550,300, 500,300, 550,250, 550,250, 550,300,
500,300, 500,300, 550,250, 550,300, 500,300,
550,250, 550,300, 550,250, 500,300, 550,250,
550,250, 550,300, 550,250, 550,250, 550,300,
500,300, 500,300, 550,250, 550,300, 500,300,
550,250, 550,300, 500,300, 500,300, 550,250,
550,250, 550,300, 500,300, 550,1000, 500,300,
500,300, 550,950, 550,1000, 500,1000, 550,1000,
500,300, 550};
unsigned int Temp29[] = {3100,1550, 600,950,
500,1000, 550,300, 500,300, 500,300, 550,950,
550,300, 550,250, 550,1000, 500,1000, 550,250,
550,1000, 500,300, 550,250, 550,950, 600,950,
550,250, 550,1000, 500,1000, 550,250, 600,250,
550,950, 550,250, 550,300, 550,950, 550,250,
550,300, 550,250, 550,250, 550,250, 550,300,
550,250, 550,250, 550,300, 500,300, 550,250,
550,250, 550,300, 500,300, 550,250, 550,250,
600,250, 550,950, 550,250, 550,300, 500,1000,
550,250, 550,300, 550,950, 550,1000, 500,300,
500,300, 550,250, 550,250, 550,300, 500,300,
550,250, 550,1000, 500,300, 550,250, 550,300,
500,300, 550,250, 550,250, 550,300, 500,1000,
550,250, 550,1000, 500,1000, 550,1000, 500,300,
500,300, 550,300, 500,300, 500,300, 550,250,
550,250, 550,300, 500,300, 500,300, 550,300,

500,300, 500,300, 550,250, 550,300, 500,300,
500,300, 550,300, 500,300, 500,300, 550,250,
550,250, 550,300, 500,300, 500,300, 550,300,
500,300, 500,300, 550,250, 550,300, 500,300,
500,300, 550,250, 550,300, 500,300, 550,250,
550,250, 550,1000, 500,1000, 550,1000, 500,1000,
550,300, 500};
unsigned int Temp30[] = {3000,1650, 500,1000,
550,1000, 500,300, 500,300, 550,250, 550,1000,
500,300, 500,300, 550,1000, 550,950, 550,250,
550,1000, 550,250, 550,250, 550,1000, 550,950,
550,300, 500,1000, 550,950, 550,300, 500,300,
550,950, 550,300, 550,250, 550,1000, 500,300,
500,300, 550,250, 550,250, 550,300, 500,300,
550,250, 550,300, 500,300, 500,300, 550,250,
550,300, 500,300, 500,300, 550,300, 500,300,
500,300, 550,950, 550,300, 500,300, 500,1000,
550,250, 550,300, 550,950, 550,1000, 500,300,
550,250, 550,250, 600,250, 500,300, 550,250,
550,1000, 500,300, 550,250, 550,300, 500,300,
500,300, 550,250, 550,300, 500,300, 550,950,
550,300, 500,1000, 550,950, 550,1000, 500,300,
550,300, 500,300, 500,300, 550,250, 550,300,
500,300, 500,300, 550,250, 550,300, 500,300,
500,300, 550,250, 550,300, 500,300, 500,300,
550,250, 550,300, 500,300, 550,250, 550,300,
500,300, 500,300, 550,250, 550,250, 550,300,
500,300, 550,250, 550,300, 500,300, 500,300,
550,250, 550,300, 500,300, 550,950, 500,1050,
500,1000, 500,350, 500,1000, 500,1000, 500,1050,

```
500,300, 500};
//Change it for your remote
IRsend irsend;
int Measured_temp;
int Measured_Humi;
int AC_Temp;
char temp_error = 2;
int Pev_value;
boolean AC = false;
int khz = 38; // 38kHz carrier frequency for the NEC
protocol
void setup()
{
Serial.begin(9600);
display.begin(SSD1306_SWITCHCAPVCC);
display.clearDisplay();
}
void loop(){

  DHT.read11(DHT11_PIN); //Read the Temp and Hu-
midity
 Measured_temp = DHT.temperature + temp_error;
 Measured_Humi = DHT.humidity;
// text display tests
 display.setTextSize(1);
 display.setTextColor(WHITE);
 display.setCursor(0,0);
  display.print("Temperature: "); display.print(Meas-
ured_temp);display.println("C");
```

```
display.setCursor(0,10);
   display.print("Humidity:  ");  display.print(Meas-
ured_Humi);display.println("%");
   display.setCursor(0,20);
  display.print("AC Temp: "); display.print(AC_Temp);
display.println("C");
   display.display();
   delay(500);
   display.clearDisplay();


   if((Measured_temp <= (Desired_temperature-3)) &&
AC == true) //If AC is turned on and temperature is less
than 3 degree of Desired value #24 turn off
   {
      irsend.sendRaw(ACoff, sizeof(ACoff) / sizeof(A-
Coff[0]), khz);  delay(2000);//Send signal to Turn Off
the AC
   AC_Temp = 0; AC=false;
   }
   if ((Measured_temp >= Desired_temperature+4) &&
AC == false) //If AC is off and measured Temp is greater
than Desired Temp
   {
      irsend.sendRaw(ACon, sizeof(ACon) / sizeof(A-
Con[0]), khz); delay(2000); //Send Signal to Turn On
the AC
   delay(2000);
    irsend.sendRaw(Temp27, sizeof(Temp27) / sizeof(
Temp27[0]), khz); //Send signal to set 27*C
```

```
    AC_Temp = 27; AC=true;
  }

  if ( Measured_temp != Pev_value) //Change the tem-
  perature only if the measured voltage value changes
  {
  if (Measured_temp == Desired_temperature+3) //If
  AC is ON and measured temp is very very high than
  desired
  {
    irsend.sendRaw(Temp24, sizeof(Temp24) / sizeof(
  Temp24[0]), khz); delay(2000);//Send signal to set
  24*C
    AC_Temp = 24;
  }
  if (Measured_temp == Desired_temperature+2) //If
  AC is ON and measured temp is very high than desired
  {
    irsend.sendRaw(Temp25, sizeof(Temp25) / sizeof(
  Temp25[0]), khz); delay(2000);//Send signal to set
  25*C
    AC_Temp = 25;
  }
  if (Measured_temp == Desired_temperature+1) //If
  AC is ON and measured temp is very high than desired
  {
    irsend.sendRaw(Temp26, sizeof(Temp26) / sizeof(
  Temp26[0]), khz); delay(2000);//Send signal to set
  26*C
    AC_Temp = 26;
  }
```

```
if (Measured_temp == 27 ) //If AC is ON and measured
temp is desired value
{
  irsend.sendRaw(Temp27, sizeof(Temp27) / sizeof(
Temp27[0]), khz); //Send signal to set 27*C
  AC_Temp = 27;
}
if (Measured_temp == Desired_temperature-1) //If AC
is ON and measured temp is low than desired value
{
  irsend.sendRaw(Temp28, sizeof(Temp28) / sizeof(
Temp28[0]), khz); delay(2000);//Send signal to set
28*C
  AC_Temp = 28;
}
if (Measured_temp == Desired_temperature-2 ) //If
AC is ON and measured temp is very low than desired
value
{
  irsend.sendRaw(Temp29, sizeof(Temp29) / sizeof(
Temp29[0]), khz); delay(2000);//Send signal to set
29*C
  AC_Temp = 29;
}
if (Measured_temp == Desired_temperature-3 ) //If
AC is ON and measured temp is very very low desired
value
{
  irsend.sendRaw(Temp30, sizeof(Temp30) / sizeof(
Temp30[0]), khz); delay(2000);//Send signal to set
```

```
30*C
 AC_Temp = 30;
}
}
Pev_value = Measured_temp;
}
```

6.ARDUINO DC MOTOR SPEED AND DIRECTION CONTROL UTILIZING RELAYS AND MOSFET

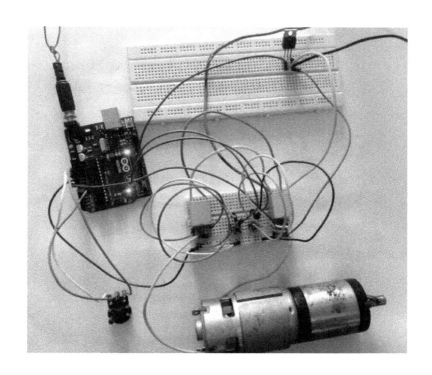

In this venture we control heading and speed of a 24v high current engine utilizing Arduino and two transfers. No power switches are required for this circuit, only two push catches and in Potentiometer to control the bearing and speed of DC Motor. One push catch will turn engine clockwise and other will pivot it counter clockwise. One n-channel MOSFET is required to control speed of engine. Transfers are utilized to switch the headings of Motor. It takes after with H-Bridge circuit.

Required Components:

- Arduino Uno
- Two 12v relay(5v relay can also be used)
- Two transistors; BC547
- Two pushbuttons
- IRF540N
- 10k resistor
- 24 volt source
- 10K potentiometer
- Three diodes 1N4007
- Connecting wires

Circuit Diagram and Explanations:

Circuit Diagram of this Bidirectional Motor Control Project is appeared in picture underneath. Make the associations as indicated by it:

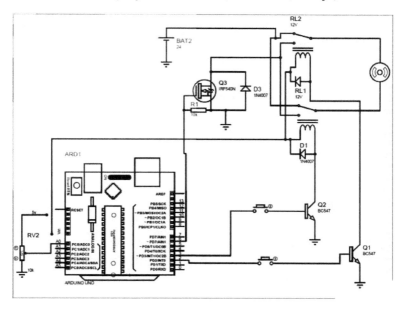

- Associate ordinarily shut terminal of the two transfers to positive terminal of battery.

- Associate regularly open terminal of both hand-off to deplete terminal of MOSFET.

- Associate wellspring of MOSFET to negative terminal of battery and to Ground stick of Arduino UNO.

- Door terminal to PWM stick 6 of Arduino.

- Associate 10k resistor from door to source and 1N4007 diode from source to deplete.

- Associate engine in the middle of the center terminal of transfers.

- Out of two residual terminals, one goes to the Vin stick of Arduino Uno and other to the authority terminal of transistor (for each hand-off).

- Associate producer terminal of both transistor to GND stick of Arduino.

- Computerized stick 2 and 3 of Arduino, every one in arrangement with pushbutton, goes to base of transistors.

- Interface diode crosswise over transfer precisely as appeared in figure.

- Interface Potentiometer's end terminal to 5v stick and Gnd stick of Arduino separately. Also, wiper terminal to A0 stick.

- ** on the off chance that you need 2 seperate 12 v battery, at that point interface one battery's sure terminal to the -ve terminal of another battery as well as utilize staying two terminals as positive and negative.

Purpose of Transistors:

Advanced pins of Arduino can't supply the measure of current expected to turn on an ordinary 5v hand-off. Other than we are utilizing 12v hand-off in this undertaking. Vin stick of Arduino can only with significant effort supply this much present for both hand-off. Thus transistors are utilized to direct current from Vin stick of Arduino to hand-off which is controlled utilizing a push-catch associated from computerized stick to base terminal of transistor.

Purpose of Arduino:

- To give the measure of current required to turn on hand-off.

- To turn on transistor.

- To control the Speed of DC Motors with Potentiometer utilizing Programming. Check the total Arduino Code toward the end.

Purpose of MOSFET:

MOSFET is necessary to control the speed of engine. MOSFET is turned on and off at high recurrence voltage and since engine is associated in arrangement with the channel of MOSFET, PWM estimation of voltage decides the speed of engine.

Current Calculations:

Obstruction of hand-off loop is estimated utilizing a multimeter which end up being = 400 ohms

Vin stick of Arduino gives = 12v

So current need to turn on the transfer = 12/400 Amps = 30 mA

In the event that the two transfers are empowered, current = 30*2 = 60 mA

**Vin stick of Arduino can supply greatest current = 200mA.

Consequently there is no over current issue in Arduino.

Working of Arduino Controlled Bi-directional Motor:

Activity of this 2-way Motor Control circuit is basic. The two pins(2 , 3) of Arduino will remain in every case high.

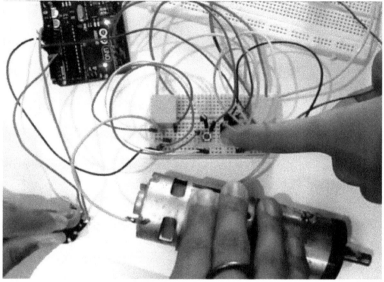

When no pushbutton is pressed:

For this situation no present streams to the base of transistor, thus transistor stays off (acts like an open switch) because of which no present streams to hand-off loop from Vin stick of Arduino.

When one push button is pressed:

For this situation some present streams to the base of

transistor through squeezed push catch which turns it on. Presently current effectively streams to transfer curl from Vin stick through this transistor which turn this hand-off (RELAY An) on and switch of this hand-off is tossed to NO position. While other transfer (RELAY B) is still in NC position. So current streams from positive terminal of battery to negative terminal through engine i.e., current streams from hand-off A to hand-off B .This causes clockwise revolution of engine.

When other push button is pressed:

This time another transfer turns on. Presently current effectively streams to transfer loop from Vin stick through transistor which turn this hand-off (RELAY B) on and switch of this hand-off is tossed to NO position. While other transfer (RELAY A) remaining parts in NC position. So current streams from positive terminal of battery to negative terminal of battery through engine. Be that as it may, this time current streams from transfer B to hand-off A. This causes anticlockwise turn of engine

When both push buttons are pressed:
For this situation current streams to the base of the two transistors because of which both transistor turns on (acts like a shut switch). What's more, along these lines both transfer is presently in NO position. So current don't spill out of positive terminal of bat-

tery to negative terminal through engine and along these lines it doesn't pivot.

Controlling the Speed of DC Motor:

Entryway of MOSFET is associated with PWM stick 6 of Arduino UNO. Mosfet is switched on and off at high PWM recurrence voltage and since engine is associated in arrangement with the channel of mosfet, PWM estimation of voltage decides the speed of engine. Presently the voltage between the wiper terminal of potentiometer and Gnd decides the PWM voltage at stick no 6 and as wiper terminal is pivoted, voltage at simple stick A0 changes causing change in speed of engine.

Code

```
int x;
int y;
void setup()
{
 pinMode(2,OUTPUT);
 pinMode(3,OUTPUT);
 pinMode(6,OUTPUT);
 pinMode(A0,INPUT);
}
void loop()
{
 x=analogRead(A0);
 y=map(x,0,1023,0,255);
```

```
analogWrite(6,y);
digitalWrite(2,HIGH);
digitalWrite(3,HIGH);
}
```

❖ ❖ ❖

7.CONTROL YOUR COMPUTER WITH HAND GESTURES UTILIZING ARDUINO

As of late Gesture controlled Laptops or PCs are getting extremely renowned. This strategy is called Leap movement which empowers us to control certain capacities on our PC/Laptop by basically waving our turn before it. It is cool and enjoyable to do it, yet these workstations are truly estimated exceptionally high. So in this task let us have a go at structure our very own Gesture control Laptop/Computer by joining the Power of Arduino and Python.

We will utilize 2 Ultrasonic sensors to decide the situation of our hand as well as control a media player (VLC) in view of the position. I have utilized this for showing, however once you have comprehended the venture, you can do anything by simply changing couple of lines of code and control your preferred application in your preferred manner.

Pre-requisites:

We have just secured few undertakings which joins Arduino with Python. So I expect that you have just introduced Python and its sequential library and have effectively evaluated couple of essential ventures like flickering LED. If not, don't stress you can fall back to this Arduino-Python Led Controlling instructional exercise and coexist with it. So ensure you have introduced Python and pyserial library before continuing.

Concept behind the project:

The idea driving the undertaking is extremely straightforward. We will put two Ultrasonic (US) sensors over our screen and will peruse the separation between the screen and our hand utilizing Arduino, in light of this estimation of separation we will play out specific activities. To perform activities on our PC we use Python pyautogui library. The directions from Arduino are sent to the PC through sequential port (USB). This information will be then perused by python which is running on the PC and dependent on the read information an activity will be performed.

Circuit Diagram:

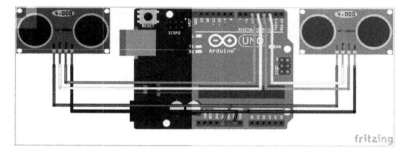

To control the PC with Hand Gestures, simply interface the 2 Ultrasonic sensors with Arduino. We know US sensor work with 5V and subsequently they are fueled by the on board Voltage controller of Arduino. The Arduino can be associated with the PC/Laptop for fueling the module and furthermore for Serial correspondence. When the associations are done place them on your screen as demonstrated as follows. I have utilized a twofold side tape to stick it on my screen however you can utilize your very own imagination. In the wake of verifying it in a spot we can continue with the Programming.

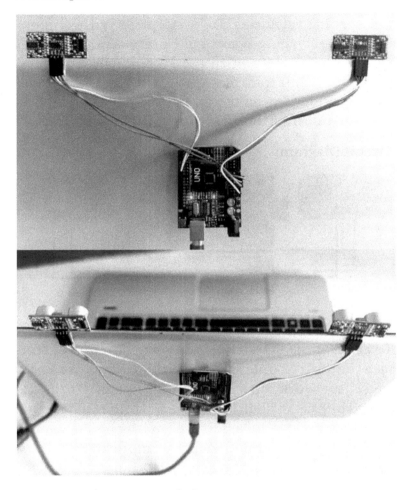

Programming your Arduino:

The Arduino ought to be modified to peruse the separation of hand from the US sensor. The total program is given toward the finish of this page; just underneath I have given the clarification for the program. In the event that you are new to Ultrasonic sensor, simply experience Arduino and Ultrasonic Sensor Based Distance Measurement.

By perusing the estimation of separation we can land at specific activities to be controlled with motions, for instance in this program I have customized 5 activities as a demo.

Activity 1: When both the hands are set up before the sensor at a specific far separation then the video in VLC player should Play/Pause.

Activity 2: When right hand is put up before the sensor at a specific far separation then the video should Fast Forward one stage.

Activity 3: When left hand is put up before the sensor at a specific far separation then the video ought to Rewind one stage.

Activity 4: When right hand is set up before the sensor at a specific close to separation and afterward whenever moved towards the sensor the video should quick advance and whenever moved away the video ought to Rewind.

Activity 5: When left hand is set up before the sensor at a specific close to separation and afterward whenever moved towards the sensor the volume of video should increment and whenever moved away the volume should Decrease.

Give us a chance to perceive how the program is composed to play out the above activities. Along these lines, similar to all projects we start with characterizing the I/O sticks as demonstrated as follows. The 2 US sensors are associated with Digital pins two,three-,four as well as five as well as are controlled by +5V stick. The trigger pins are yield stick as well as Echo pins are information pins.

The Serial correspondence among Arduino and python takes places at a baud pace of 9600.

```
const int trigger1 = 2; //Trigger pin of 1st Sesnor

const int echo1 = 3; //Echo pin of 1st Sesnor

const int trigger2 = 4; //Trigger pin of 2nd Sesnor

const int echo2 = 5;//Echo pin of 2nd Sesnor

void setup() {

Serial.begin(9600);

pinMode(trigger1, OUTPUT);

pinMode(echo1, INPUT);

pinMode(trigger2, OUTPUT);
```

```
pinMode(echo2, INPUT);

}
```

We have to compute the separation between the Sensor as well as the hand each time before closing on any activity. So we need to do it commonly, which means this code ought to be utilized as a capacity. We have composed a capacity named calculate_distance() which will return us the separation between the sensor as well as the hand.

```
/*###Function to calculate distance###*/

void calculate_distance(int trigger, int echo)

{

digitalWrite(trigger, LOW);

delayMicroseconds(2);

digitalWrite(trigger, HIGH);

delayMicroseconds(10);

digitalWrite(trigger, LOW);

time_taken = pulseIn(echo, HIGH);
```

```
dist= time_taken*0.034/2;

if(dist>50)

dist = 50;

}
```

Inside our principle circle we check for the estimation of separation and play out the activities referenced previously. Before that we utilize two factors distL and distR which gets refreshed with current separation esteem.

```
calculate_distance(trigger1,echo1);

distL =dist; //get distance of left sensor

calculate_distance(trigger2,echo2);

distR =dist; //get distance of right sensor
```

Since we know the separation between both the sensors, we would now be able to contrast it and predefined values and land at specific activities. For instance on the off chance that both the hands are put a ways off of 40 mc, at that point we play/delay the video. Here "Play/Pause" will be conveyed through sequential port

```
if ((distL >40 && distR>40) && (distL <50 &&
distR<50)) //Detect both hands

{Serial.println("Play/Pause"); delay (500);}
```

On the off chance that the Right hand alone is put before the module, at that point we quick forward the video by one stage and on the off chance that it is left hand we rewind by one stage. In light of the activity, here "Rewind" or "Forward" will be conveyed through sequential port

```
if ((distL >40 && distL<50) && (distR ==50)) //De-
tect Left Hand

{Serial.println("Rewind"); delay (500);}

if ((distR >40 && distR<50) && (distL ==50)) //De-
tect Right Hand

{Serial.println("Forward"); delay (500);}
```

Enemy point by point control of volume and track we utilize an alternate strategy in order to counteract false triggers. To control the volume we need to put the left hand approx. A good ways off of 15 cm , then you can either move it towards the sensor to diminish the volume of move it away from the sensor to build the volume. The code for the equivalent is demonstrated as follows. In light of the activity, here "Vup" or "Vdown" will be conveyed through sequential port

```
//Lock Left - Control Mode

if(distL>=13 && distL<=17)

{

    delay(100); //Hand Hold Time

    calculate_distance(trigger1,echo1);

    distL =dist;

    if(distL>=13 && distL<=17)

    {

        Serial.println("Left Locked");

        while(distL<=40)

        {

            calculate_distance(trigger1,echo1);
```

```
distL =dist;

if (distL < 10) //Hand pushed in

{Serial.println ("Vup"); delay (300);}

if (distL > 20) //Hand pulled out

{Serial.println ("Vdown"); delay (300);}

  }

 }

}
```

We can utilize a similar strategy for the correct side sensor additionally, to control the track of the video. That is on the off chance that we move the correct hand towards the sensor it will quick advance the film and on the off chance that you move it away from the sensor it will rewind the motion picture. In light of the activity, here "Rewind" or "Forward" will be conveyed through sequential port

You would now be able to peruse the total code for this motion controlled PC given toward the finish of the page and take a stab at downplaying it as an entire and afterward duplicate it to your Arduino IDE.

Programming your Python:

The python program for this venture is exceptionally basic. We simply need to set up a sequential correspondence with Arduino through the right baud rate and after that play out some essential console activities. The initial step with python is introduce the pyautogui module. Ensure you pursue this progression in light of the fact that the program won't work without pyautogui module.

Installing pyautogui module for windows:

Pursue the beneath steps to introduce pyautogui for windows. In case you are utilizing different stages the means will likewise be pretty much comparable. Ensure your PC/Laptop is associated with web and continue with steps underneath

Stage 1: Open Windows Command brief and change the catalog to the organizer where you have introduced python. As a matter of course the direction ought to be

```
cd C:\Python27
```

Stage 2: Inside your python registry utilize the direction python – m pip introduce – overhaul pip to update your pip. Pip is an apparatus in python which causes us to introduce python modules effectively. When this module is redesigned (as appeared in picture beneath) continue to following stage.

python –m pip install –upgrade pip

Stage 3: Use the order "python – m pip introduce pyautogui" to introduce the pyautogui module.
When the procedure is effective you should see a
screen something like this underneath.

python –m pip install –upgrade pip

Presently that the pyautogui module and pyserial

module (introduced in past instructional exercise) is fruitful introduced with the python, we can continue with the python program. The total python code is given toward the finish of the instructional exercise yet the clarification for the equivalent is as per the following.

Give us a chance to import all the three required modules for this venture. They are pyautogui, sequential python and time.

```
import serial #Serial imported for Serial commu-
nication

import time #Required to use delay functions

import pyautogui
```

Next we build up association with the Arduino through COM port. In my PC the Arduino is associated with COM 18. Use gadget supervisor to discover to which COM port your Arduino is associated with and right the accompanying line in like manner.

```
ArduinoSerial = serial.Serial('com18',9600) #Cre-
ate Serial port object called arduinoSerialData

time.sleep(2) #wait for 2 seconds for the communi-
```

cation to get established

Inside the unbounded while circle, we more than once tune in to the COM port and contrast the watchwords and any pre-resisted works and make console presses in like manner.

```
while 1:

    incoming = str (ArduinoSerial.readline()) #read the serial data and print it as line

    print incoming

    if 'Play/Pause' in incoming:

        pyautogui.typewrite(['space'], 0.2)

    if 'Rewind' in incoming:

        pyautogui.hotkey('ctrl', 'left')

    if 'Forward' in incoming:

        pyautogui.hotkey('ctrl', 'right')

    if 'Vup' in incoming:

        pyautogui.hotkey('ctrl', 'down')
```

```
if 'Vdown' in incoming:

    pyautogui.hotkey('ctrl', 'up')
```

As should be obvious, to press a key we just need to utilize the order "pyautogui.typewrite(['space'], 0.2)" which will press the key space for 0.2 sec. In case you need hot keys like ctrl+S, at that point you can utilize the hot key direction "pyautogui.hotkey('ctrl', 's')".

I have utilized these mixes in light of the fact that they chip away at VLC media player you can change them in any capacity you like to make your own applications to control anything in PC with motions.

Gesture Controlled Computer in Action:

Make the associations as characterized above and transfer the Arduino code on your Arduino board. At that point utilize the python content beneath and dispatch the program on your workstation/PC.

Presently you can play any motion picture on your PC utilizing the VLC media player and utilize your hand to control the film.

Expectation you comprehended the task and de-lighted in playing with it. This is only a demo and you can utilize your inventiveness to manufacture significantly increasingly cool motion controlled stuff around this. Fill me in as to whether this was helpful and what you will make utilizing this in the remark area and I will be glad to know it.

Code

Arduino Code:

```
/*
* Program for gesture control VLC Player
*/
const int trigger1 = 2; //Trigger pin of 1st Sesnor
```

```
const int echo1 = 3; //Echo pin of 1st Sesnor
const int trigger2 = 4; //Trigger pin of 2nd Sesnor
const int echo2 = 5;//Echo pin of 2nd Sesnor
long time_taken;
int dist,distL,distR;
void setup() {
Serial.begin(9600);

pinMode(trigger1, OUTPUT);
pinMode(echo1, INPUT);
pinMode(trigger2, OUTPUT);
pinMode(echo2, INPUT);
}
/*###Function to calculate distance###*/
void calculate_distance(int trigger, int echo)
{
digitalWrite(trigger, LOW);
delayMicroseconds(2);
digitalWrite(trigger, HIGH);
delayMicroseconds(10);
digitalWrite(trigger, LOW);
time_taken = pulseIn(echo, HIGH);
dist= time_taken*0.034/2;
if(dist>50)
dist = 50;
}
void loop() { //infinite loopy
calculate_distance(trigger1,echo1);
distL =dist; //get distance of left sensor
```

```
calculate_distance(trigger2,echo2);
distR =dist; //get distance of right sensor
//Uncomment for debudding
/*Serial.print("L=");
Serial.println(distL);
Serial.print("R=");
Serial.println(distR);
*/
//Pause Modes -Hold
if ((distL >40 && distR>40) && (distL <50 &&
distR<50)) //Detect both hands
{Serial.println("Play/Pause"); delay (500);}
calculate_distance(trigger1,echo1);
distL =dist;
calculate_distance(trigger2,echo2);
distR =dist;
//Control Modes
//Lock Left - Control Mode
if(distL>=13 && distL<=17)
{
 delay(100); //Hand Hold Time
 calculate_distance(trigger1,echo1);
 distL =dist;
 if(distL>=13 && distL<=17)
 {
  Serial.println("Left Locked");
  while(distL<=40)
  {
   calculate_distance(trigger1,echo1);
   distL =dist;
```

```
  if(distL<10) //Hand pushed in
  {Serial.println ("Vup"); delay (300);}
  if(distL>20) //Hand pulled out
  {Serial.println ("Vdown"); delay (300);}
  }
 }
}
//Lock Right - Control Mode
if(distR>=13 && distR<=17)
{
 delay(100); //Hand Hold Time
 calculate_distance(trigger2,echo2);
 distR =dist;
 if(distR>=13 && distR<=17)
 {
  Serial.println("Right Locked");
  while(distR<=40)
  {
   calculate_distance(trigger2,echo2);
   distR =dist;
   if(distR<10) //Right hand pushed in
   {Serial.println ("Rewind"); delay (300);}
   if(distR>20) //Right hand pulled out
   {Serial.println ("Forward"); delay (300);}
  }
 }
}
delay(200);
}
```

Python Code:

```python
import serial #Serial imported for Serial communication
import time #Required to use delay functions
import pyautogui
ArduinoSerial = serial.Serial('com18',9600) #Create
Serial port object called arduinoSerialData
time.sleep(2) #wait for 2 seconds for the communication to get established
while 1:
    incoming = str (ArduinoSerial.readline()) #read the
serial data and print it as line
    print incoming


    if 'Play/Pause' in incoming:
        pyautogui.typewrite(['space'], 0.2)
    if 'Rewind' in incoming:
        pyautogui.hotkey('ctrl', 'left')
    if 'Forward' in incoming:
        pyautogui.hotkey('ctrl', 'right')
    if 'Vup' in incoming:
        pyautogui.hotkey('ctrl', 'down')


    if 'Vdown' in incoming:
        pyautogui.hotkey('ctrl', 'up')
    incoming = "";
```

Anbazhagan K

8.AUTOMATIC CALL REPLYING MAIL UTILIZING ARDUINO AND GSM MODULE

In the present current world we as a whole rely upon cell phones as our essential methods for remote correspondence. Yet, we as a whole have confronted circumstances during which we probably won't have the option to reply to our calls, these calls may be a significant individual call or an extraordinary business call and you could have recently botched that chance since you were not ready to answer that call at that specific time.

This venture means to take care of this issue by making an Automatic Call replying mail by utilizing Arduino and GSM module. Next time when you are changing to another telephone number or out for a long journey trip or getting a charge out of a merited get-away simply utilize this machine to record your voice expressing the explanation behind nonattendance and every one of your calls will be naturally replied by this machine and your recorded voice will be played to them. This can likewise be utilized for your business numbers to reply to your client's calls during non-available time. Sounds intriguing right? So let us fabricate it..

Materials Required:

The undertaking may sound somewhat confounded yet it is extremely simple to manufacture, you simply need the accompanying segments

- Arduino Uno

- GSM module – Flyscale SIM 900

- ISD 1820 Voice Module

- 12V connector to control GSM module

- 9V battery to control Arduino

- Associating wires

Before we really continue into the task, let us get acquainted with the GSM module and ISD 1820 Voice Module

Fly Scale SIM900 GSM Module:

GSM modules are interesting to utilize particularly when our venture requires remote access. These modules could make all activities that our typical cell phone could do, such as making/getting a call, sending/accepting a SMS, associating with web utilizing GPRS and so forth. You can likewise associate a typical receiver and speaker to this module and banter on your versatile calls. Here are a few instructional exercises on them utilizing distinctive microcontroller:

- Call and Message utilizing Arduino as well as GSM Module

- Call and Text utilizing Raspberry Pi and GSM Module

- GSM module Interfacing with PIC Microcontroller - Make and Receive Calls

As appeared in beneath pic the GSM module accompanies a USART connector which can be straightforwardly interfaced to the PC by utilizing a MAX232 module or the Tx and Rx pins can be utilized to combine it to a Microcontroller. You can likewise see different pins like MIC+, MIC-, SP+, SP-and so forth where an amplifier or a Speaker can be associated. The module can be fueled by a 12V connector through a typical DC barrel jack.

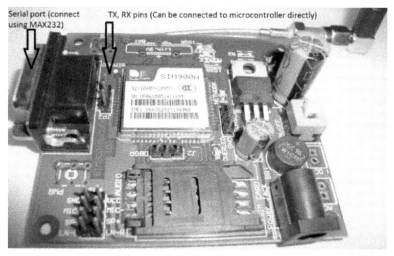

Serial port (connect using MAX232)

TX, RX pins (Can be connected to microcontroller directly)

GSM Module SIM900A

Supplement your SIM card in the opening of the module and power it on, you should see a power LED going ON. Presently sit tight for a moment or somewhere in the vicinity, and you should see a red (or some other shading) LED Flashing once for at regular intervals. This implies your Module was proficient to build up association with your SIM card. Presently you can continue with associating you module with Phone or any Microcontroller.

ISD1820 Voice module:

The ISD 1820 Voice module is extremely a cool module that could zest up your Projects with Voice declarations. This module is equipped for chronicle an Audio cut for 10 seconds and afterward playing it when required. The module itself accompanies an amplifier and a speaker (8ohms 0.5watts) and it should look something like this demonstrated as follows.

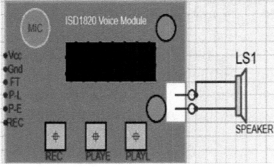

The module chips away at +5V and can be fueled utilizing the berg sticks on the left. It likewise has three catches at the base which are Rec. catch, PlayE. catch and PlayL. catch separately. You can record your voice by squeezing the Rec. catch and play it utilizing the PlayE catch. The PlayL will play the voice as long as you hold the catch. When interfacing with a MCU, we can utilize the pins on the left. These pins are 3V-5V average and subsequently can be straightforwardly determined by Arduino/ESP8266. Here we are controlling the PLAYE stick utilizing the D8 stick of our Arduino module. With the goal that we can play the recorded voice when a call is distinguished and gotten by the GSM module.

Circuit Diagram and Explanation:

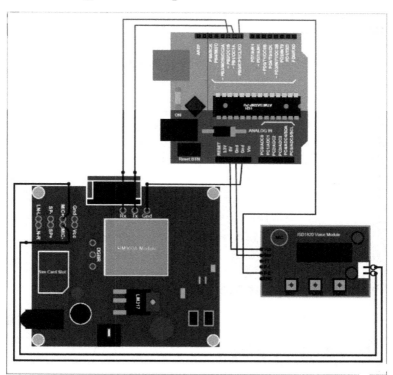

The total circuit outline of this Automatic Voice Call replying mail venture is given previously. As should be obvious the associations are extremely basic. We control the GSM module with a 12V 1A connector and Arduino with 9V battery, the ISD Voice module is fueled by the +5V stick of the Arduino. As we probably am aware we can record anything on our voice module by squeezing the rec catch and this will get played when P-E is squeezed, this sound must be sent to the mouthpiece of the GSM module. So we associate the speaker stick of the Voice module to the amplifier stick of the GSM module.

Here, the Arduino and GSM module is interface sequentially, the Tx stick of Arduino is combined with stick 9 and Rx stick is associated stick 10. This will assist the Arduino with listening to the GSM module. At the point when a call lands to the GSM module the Arduino will hear it out and request that the GSM module answer the call. The Arduino ensures that the consider is dynamic and afterward plays the recorded voice message on the voice module by making the stick 8 (Connected to P-E of voice module) go high for 200ms.

Programming your Arduino:

We know from the above passage what is the job of Arduino here is; presently given us a chance to investigate the code which does likewise. The total Arduino code of the undertaking is given at the base of this page, further here I have spilt the code into little trashes to clarify it.

Before we go before any further introduce the GSM Library, benevolently click on this Github GSM library connect to download the library utilized in this undertaking. You will get a compress document which must be added to your Arduino library by Sketch - > Include Librarey - > Add .Zip record.

The initial three lines of the code appeared beneath are utilized to incorporate the library to our code. We utilize the sequential library and wire library since we are not utilizing the default Rx and Tx pins of the Arduino to speak with GSM module.

```
#include <sim900.h> //download librarey from https://github.com/Seeed-Studio/GPRS_SIM900

#include <SoftwareSerial.h> //default librarey

#include <Wire.h> //default library
```

We empower sequential correspondence on pins 9 and 10 utilizing the accompanying line. This is made conceivable by the product sequential library that we included previously.

```
SoftwareSerial gprs(9,10);//TX,RX
```

Inside our arrangement work, we introduce the sequential screen at 9600 baud rate and GSM module is likewise instated with 9600 Baudrate. The stick 8 which triggers the voice is announced as yield stick.

```
void setup(){

    Serial.begin(9600); //Serial monitor works on
9600 baudrate for debugging

    sim900_init(&gprs, 9600); //GSM module works
on 9600 baudrate

    pinMode(8, OUTPUT); //pin to turn on Voice

    Serial.println("Arduino - Automatic Voice Machine");

}
```

Next we need to make a capacity that could peruse and comprehend what the GSM module is stating through its Serial port. In the event that we utilize straightforward sequential read line like "gprs.read()" to peruse the message we will get them in type of

ASCII decimal qualities, this will look bad to us.

So the accompanying capacity is utilized to change over these decimal qualities to strings by utilizing string items and after that link them to shape a string. The last string worth is put away in the variable Fdata, which is of sort string and can be utilized to contrast and any String qualities.

```
void check_Incoming()

{

    if(gprs.available()) //If GSM is saying something

    {

    Incomingch = gprs.read(); // Listen to it and store
in this variable

    if (Incomingch == 10 || Incomingch ==13) //If it
says space (10) or Newline (13) it means it has com-
pleted one word

    {Serial.println(data);  Fdata =data; data = ""; } //
Print the word and clear the variable to start fresh

    else
```

Anbazhagan K

```
{

String newchar = String (char(Incomingch)); //
convert the char to string by using string objects

data = data +newchar; // After converting to
string, do string concatenation

}

}

}
```

The accompanying lines are utilized for investigating, with these debugger lines you can send any AT directions from the Serial screen of Arduino to GSM and furthermore observe what is reactions on the sequential screen.

```
if(Serial.available()){ //Used for debugging

gprs.write(Serial.read()); //Used for debugging

} //Used for debugging
```

As said before, the Arduino needs to check if the GSM module is getting any calls. This should be possible by making the Arduino to check for "RING" on the grounds that the GSM module will yield RING in case of a call as per the AT direction list. When it finds a call it will sit tight for 5 seconds and send the direction "ATA" to the GSM module, this will make the GSM module to answer the call and in the wake of noting it will react with "alright". The Arduino again sits tight for the "alright" affirmation and after that turns the in Pin 8 high for 200ms to play the recorded voice from voice module.

---

if (Fdata == "RING") //If the GSM module says RING

{

delay(5000); //wait for 5 sec to create 3 ring delay.

gprs.write ("ATA\r\n"); //Answer the call

Serial.println ("Placed Received"); //Used for debugging

while(Fdata != "OK") //Until call successfully answered

{check_Incoming(); //Read what GSM modue is saying

Serial.println ("Playing Recorded message"); //Used for debugging

---

```
//Play the recored voice message

delay(500);

digitalWrite(8, HIGH); //Go high

delay(200);   // wait for 200 msec

digitalWrite(8, LOW); //Go low

}
```

Working:

When your code and equipment is prepared, it is the ideal opportunity for some good times. Power both the modules and press the REC catch on the Voice module and record a message. This message must be of 10 seconds in length.

Presently program your Arduino utilizing the under-neath given code and supplement the SIM vehicle in the GSM module, you should hang tight for in any event 2 minutes now so the GSM module could set up association with your Network specialist co-op. When done you should see a red shading LED blazing once for like clockwork, this shows your SIM is pre-pared to accept calls. You would now be able to have a go at calling to this SIM card from any number and you ought to hear the recorded message after three persistent rings.

Tadaaaaaa!!! Presently you have your own Automatic voice call replying mail and simply feel free to utilize it when required and stun your loved ones with it.

Expectation you delighted in the undertaking and

construct something comparable, If you had any issues post them on the remark area and I will enable you to out.

Code

```
/*
Automatic Voice machine using Arudino and GSM900
*/
#include <sim900.h>      //download library from https://github.com/Seeed-Studio/GPRS_SIM900
#include <SoftwareSerial.h> //default library
#include <Wire.h> //default library
int Incomingch;
String data,Fdata;
//Connect Tx pin of GSM to 9 of Arduino
//Connect Rx pin of GSM to 10 of Arduino
SoftwareSerial gprs(9,10);//TX,RX
void setup(){
  Serial.begin(9600); //Serial monitor works on 9600 baudrate for debugging
  sim900_init(&gprs, 9600); //GSM module works on 9600 baudrate
 pinMode(8, OUTPUT); //pin to turn on Voice
   Serial.println("Arduino - Automatic Voice Machine");
}
/*Function to read Incoming data from GSM to Ar-
```

```
duino*/
void check_Incoming()
{
  if(gprs.available()) //If GSM is saying something
  {
  Incomingch = gprs.read(); // Listen to it and store in
this variable


  if (Incomingch == 10 || Incomingch ==13) //If it says
space (10) or Newline (13) it means it has completed
one word
  {Serial.println(data);  Fdata =data; data = ""; } //Print
the word and clear the variable to start fresh
  else
  {
  String newchar = String (char(Incomingch)); //con-
vert the char to string by using string objects
  data = data +newchar; // After converting to string,
do string concatenation
  }
  }
}
/*##End of Function##*/
void loop(){


  check_Incoming(); //Read what GSM module is say-
ing
```

```
if(Serial.available()){ //Used for debugging
gprs.write(Serial.read()); //Used for debugging
} //Used for debugging
if (Fdata == "RING") //If the GSM module says RING
{
delay(5000); //wait for 5 sec to create 3 ring delay.
gprs.write ("ATA\r\n"); //Answer the call
Serial.println ("Placed Received"); //Used for debug-
ging
    while(Fdata != "OK") //Until call successfully an-
swered
{check_Incoming(); //Read what GSM module is say-
ing
Serial.println ("Playing Recorded message"); //Used
for debugging
//Play the recorded voice message
delay(500);
digitalWrite(8, HIGH); //Go high
delay(200);   // wait for 200 msec
digitalWrite(8, LOW); //Go low
}
}
}
```

9.INTERFACING ARDUINO WITH VPYTHON - CREATING GRAPHICS

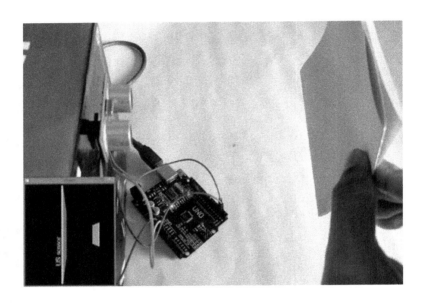

In our past instructional exercise we figured out how to introduce python on our windows machine and how to interface Arduino with python utilizing a basic LED control venture. In case you are new, I would emphatically prescribe you to fall back to the past instructional exercise since this instructional exercise is a continuation of the equivalent.

You may have just begun to ask why we would require python with Arduino if all that it could do is basically convey over sequential port. In any case, Python is solid advancement stage on which a great deal of cool applications wherein AI, PC vision and significantly more can be incorporated. In this instructional exercise we will figure out How we can Create a Small Graphical Interface Using Python. To do this we will require a module called Vpython. The accompanying instructional exercise is material just for windows client since for Mac or Linux client, the system is extraordinary.

End of this instructional exercise we will figure out how we can make basic GUI utilizing Python. We will make a little liveliness which reacts to the estimation of Ultrasonic sensor that is joined to the Arduino. This application tracks the item utilizing Ultrasonic sensor and showcases it in Graphical structure on PC utilizing VPython. As we move the item, Ultrasonic sensor detects the separation and sends this data to Python program utilizing Arduino and it will move the article in the PC as well. Sounds fascinating right! So let begin...

Pre-requisites:

- Arduino (Any version)

- Learning on past instructional exercise

Anbazhagan K

- Associating Wires

- Ultrasonic Sensor HC-SR04

- PC with Python

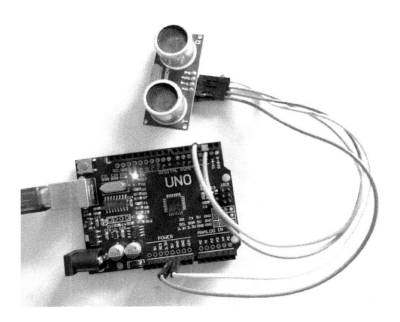

Installing VPython on your Computer:

In our past instructional exercise we have as of now figured out how to introduce python on your machine and how to move around it and make a basic program with Arduino. Presently we have introduce Visual Python (VPython) over this so we can make cool Graphics utilizing Python for Arduino. For the

166

straightforward strides underneath to begin with VPython

Stage 1. Ensure Python is as of now introduced according to past instructional exercise rules.

Stage 2. Snap on VPython to download the exe document for Visual Python. Try not to pick to introduce a 64–piece form regardless of whether your machine keeps running on 64-piece. Simply pursue the connection given.

Stage 3. Dispatch the exe document and pursue the arrangement. Try not to change the default index way and ensure you have chosen "full establishment".

Stage 4. Once introduced, you should locate another application named "VIDLE(VPython)" on your work area or application board as demonstrated as follows.

Note: VIDLE for VPython is unique in relation to IDLE for python

Stage 5. Dispatch the application and you ought to get a window as demonstrated as follows.

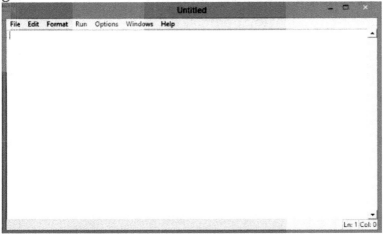

Stage 6. This is where we will type in the program for

VPython. Be that as it may, until further notice let us check if Vpython is working by opening a model program. To do this select File->Open->Bounce

Stage 7. You ought to get a model program opened. Take a stab at propelling the program utilizing Run -> Run Module. In case everything is filling in true to form you ought to get the accompanying screen.

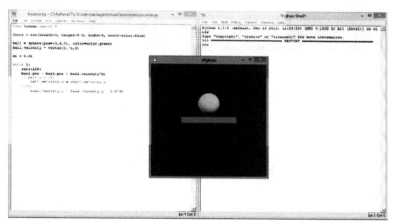

You should see the Shell window (left) with two >>> demonstrating effective assemblage and the real window (front) which demonstrates a ball ricocheting.

Stage 8. You can likewise attempt other model projects to find the intensity of VPython, for example the model program called "electric-engine" will dumbfound you by the accompanying screen.

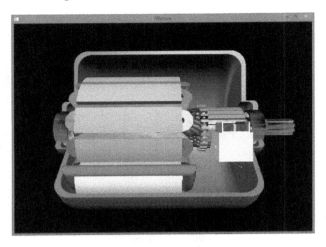

Stage 9. This implies your VPython is prepared for use and you can tumble down to the "Programming your Vpython" subject.

Stage 10. Else in the event that you resemble one among the numerous who get a "numpy Error" don't lose trust in we will deal with that issue in the further advances

Stage 11. Open My PC - > C drive - > Python 27 - > Scripts - > local.bat. This will dispatch a direction expeditious as demonstrated as follows

Stage 12. Presently type "pip introduce - update numpy" and press enter. The new form of Numpy ought to get introduced on your machine. You may need to hang tight for quite a while if your web association is moderate.

Stage 13. When done you can fall back to step number 4 and attempt a model program and you ought to have the option to make it work.

Programming VPython:

Next start programming into our VPython window. In this program we will make two 3D rectangular items one will be set in the focal point of the screen reference to the stationary Ultrasonic sensor and the other will be at a powerful area dependent on the separation among the US sensor and the article (paper).

The total Python code can be found toward the finish of this page. Further down, I have clarified this python code by parting them into little important throws out.

The primary line is import the visual Library with the goal that we can make 3D objects. The beneath line does likewise.

from visual import *

You ought to be acquainted with the following four lines, since we have utilized them as of now in our past instructional exercise. They are utilized to import Serial and time library and furthermore set up a sequential association with Arduino at COM18 with 9600 as baudrate

import serial #Serial imported for Serial communication

import time #Required to use delay functions

ArduinoSerial = serial.Serial('com18',9600) #Create Serial port object called arduinoSerialData

time.sleep(2) #wait for 2 secounds for the communication to get established

Presently, the time has come to make objects. I have made two 3d square shapes named as obj and divider. The wallL is a stationary divider in cyan shading put at the focal point of the screen and the obj is the versatile item in white shading. I have additionally put a book "US sensor" close to the divider object.

```
obj     =     box(pos=(-5,0,0),     size=(0.1,4,4),
color=color.white)

wallL   =     box(pos=(-1,0,0),     size=(0.2,12,12),
color=color.cyan)

text(text='US sensor', axis=(0,1,0) , pos=(-2,-6,0),
depth=-0.3, color=color.cyan)
```

I am certain that the over three lines would have showed up as Greek and Latin for the greater part of the first run through perusers, yet with time you would have the option to get it. Everything that is referenced inside sections is (x,y,z) co-ordinates. What's more, these co-ordinates are fundamentally the same as the ones that we find in our secondary school geometry class as demonstrated as follows.

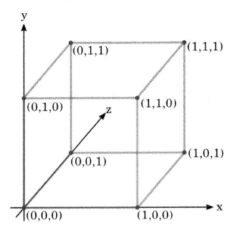

Presently, the illustrations and sequential port is prepared all that we need to do is perused the information and spot the "obj" (white square shape) in a spot as per the information originating from the Arduino. This should be possible by the accompanying lines, where obj.pos.x controls the X- axis position of the item (White square shape).

```
t = int (ArduinoSerial.readline()) #read the serial
data and print it as line

t = t* 0.05

obj.pos.x = t
```

Getting your Arduino Ready:

The Python content is prepared to tune in for qualities from COM port and energize the illustrations as needs be, yet our Arduino isn't prepared at this point. Initially we need to interface the Ultrasonic sensor to the Arduino as indicated by the accompanying Circuit Diagram. On the off chance that you are totally new to US sensor and Arduino, at that point you need to fall back to Arduino and Ultrasonic Sensor Based Distance Measurement instructional exercise.

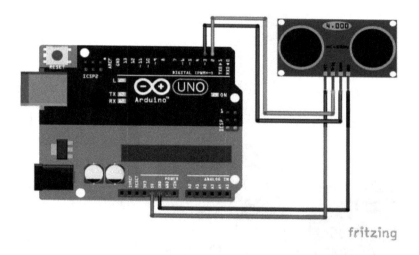

fritzing

At that point transfer the Arduino Program given toward the finish of this page. The program is self clarified utilizing remark lines. We realize that ultrasonic sensor works by figuring the time taken for the beat to hit an item and return back. This worth is determined by utilizing the PulseIn work in Arduino. Later the time taken is changed over into separation utilizing the beneath line.

```
dist = (timetaken/2) / 2.91;
```

Here the separation is determined as far as milli-meters (mm).

Working:

The working of the task is basic. Dispatch the Python program and spot an item before the US sensor as demonstrated as follows:

Presently dispatch the python program and you

ought to have the option to see the white square shape move alongside your paper, the separation between your paper and sensor will likewise be shown in the shell window as show in the picture beneath.

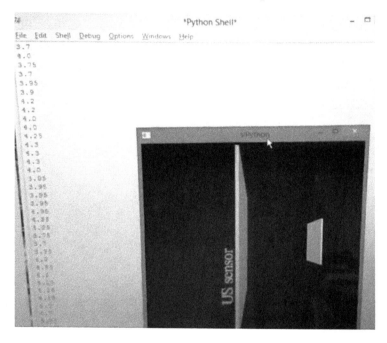

This is the way we can follow the movement of item utilizing Ultrasonic sensor and Python with Arduino.

Expectation you comprehended the undertaking and delighted in structure one. This is only one inconspicuous advance towards python yet you can construct significantly increasingly innovative things utilizing this. See you with another fascinating python venture.

Code

Python Code:

```
from visual import *
import serial #Serial imported for Serial communication
import time #Required to use delay functions
ArduinoSerial = serial.Serial('com18',9600) #Create Serial port object called arduinoSerialData
time.sleep(2) #wait for 2 secounds for the communication to get established
obj       =       box(pos=(-5,0,0),       size=(0.1,4,4), color=color.white)
wallL     =       box(pos=(-1,0,0),       size=(0.2,12,12), color=color.cyan)
text(text='US sensor', axis=(0,1,0) , pos=(-2,-6,0), depth=-0.3, color=color.cyan)
t = 0
while 1:
  rate(100)
    t = int (ArduinoSerial.readline()) #read the serial data and print it as line
  t= t*0.05
  obj.pos.x = t
  print(t)
```

Arduino Code:

```
#define Trigger 2
#define Echo 3
int timetaken, dist;
```

```
int sendv;
void setup() {
 Serial.begin (9600);
 pinMode(Trigger, OUTPUT);
 pinMode(Echo, INPUT);
}
void loop() {
 timetaken=dist=0; //initialize the variable to zero
before calculation
 //request the US to send a wave
 digitalWrite(Trigger, HIGH);
 digitalWrite(Trigger, LOW);


 timetaken = pulseIn(Echo, HIGH); //calculate the
time taken for the wave to return
 dist = (timetaken/2) / 2.91; //formulae to calculate
the distance using time taken


 if (dist <= 200 && dist > 0)//send the value to py-
thon only if it ranhes from 0-20 cm
 sendv = dist;
 Serial.println(sendv);


 delay(200);


}
```

Anbazhagan K

❖ ❖ ❖

10.ARDUINO BASED FLOOR CLEANING ROBOT UTILIZING ULTRASONIC SENSOR

Programmed floor cleaners are the same old thing, however they all offer a typical issue. They all are unreasonably costly for what they do. An Automatic Home cleaning Robot that solitary costs a little division of the ones in the market. This Robot can recognize the snags and articles before it and can keep moving, maintaining a strategic distance from the impediments, until the entire room is cleaned. It has a little brush connected to it to clean the floor.

Likewise check our Smart Vacuum Cleaning Robot utilizing Arduino

Component Required:

- Battery for the Motors.
- Arduino UNO R3.
- Arduino Motor Driver shield.
- Wheel Drive Robot Chassis.
- Ultrasonic Sensor.
- Computer to Program the Arduino.
- A Scotch Brite Scrub Pad.
- A Shoe Brush.
- A Power Bank To Power The Arduino

Note: Instead of utilizing batteries, you can likewise utilize a long 4-stranded wire as we did. Despite the fact that this is certainly not an extremely exquisite or down to earth arrangement however you can do in case you're not intending to utilize it in reality consistently. Ensure the link's lengths are sufficient.

Before broadly expounding lets talk about Ultrasonic first.

HC-SR04 Ultrasonic Sensor:

The Ultrasonic Sensor is used to gauge the separation with high exactness and stable readings. It can quantify good ways since 2cm to 400cm or since 1 inch to 13 feet. It discharges a ultrasound wave at the recurrence of 40KHz noticeable all around and in case the article will come in its manner, at that point it will ricochet back to the sensor. By utilizing that time which it takes to strike the item and returns, you can figure the separation.

The ultrasonic sensor utilizes a strategy called "Reverberation". "Reverberation" is basically a reflected sound wave. You will have an ECHO when sound reflects back in the wake of arriving at an impasse.

HCSR04 module creates a sound vibration in ultrasonic range when we make the 'Trigger' stick high for about 10us which will send a eight cycle sonic burst at the speed of sound and in the wake of striking the item, it will be gotten by the Echo stick. Contingent upon time taken by sound vibration to get back, it gives fitting heartbeat yield. In the event that the item is far away, at that point it requires some investment for ECHO to be heard and the yield beat width will be huge. What's more, in case the obstruction is close, at that point the ECHO will be heard quicker and yield beat width will be littler.

We can compute the separation of the article dependent on the time taken by ultrasonic wave to return back to the sensor. Since the time and speed of sound is realized we can compute the separation by the accompanying formulae.

Distance= (Time x Speed of Sound in Air (343 m/ s))/2.

The worth is isolated by two since the wave goes ahead and in reverse covering a similar separation. Subsequently an opportunity to arrive at impediment is simply a large portion of the absolute time taken

So Distance in centimeter = 17150*T

We have recently made numerous valuable undertaking utilizing this Ultrasonic sensor and Arduino, check them underneath:

- Arduino Based Distance Measurement utilizing Ultrasonic Sensor

- Entryway Alarm utilizing Arduino and Ultrasonic Sensor

- IOT Based Dumpster Monitoring utilizing Arduino

Assembly of Floor Cleaner Robot:

Mount the Arduino on the frame. Ensure you don't impede on the off chance that your suspension is made of metal. It is a smart thought to get a case for the Arduino and the engine controller shield. Secure the engines with the haggles utilizing screws. Your frame ought to have choices to do this from the processing plant, yet in the event that it doesn't, you can ad lib an alternate arrangement. Epoxy is certifiably not an impractical notion. Mount the shoe brush on the facade of the case. We utilized a mix of M-Seal epoxy and bored screws for this, however you can utilize whatever other arrangement that may be simpler for you. Mount the Scotch Brite clean cushion behind the brush. We utilized a pole going over the body that holds it in play, however this is improvisable also. A spring stacked shaft can be utilized to go with it. Mount the batteries (or links on the back of the skeleton). Epoxy or a battery holder are great approaches to do this. Craft glue isn't awful either.

Wiring and Connections:

Circuit for this Automatic Home Cleaning Robot is exceptionally straightforward. Associate the Ultrasonic sensor to the Arduino as referenced underneath and place the Motor Driver shield on to the Arduino like some other shield.

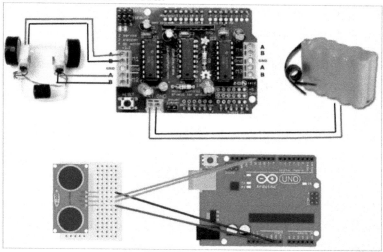

The Trig stick of Ultrasonic is associated with the twelfth stick on the Arduino, the Echo stick is associated with the thirteenth stick, the voltage stick to the 5 V stick and the Ground stick to the ground stick. The Echo stick and the Trig stick enable the Arduino to speak with the sensor. Power is conveyed to the sensor through the voltage and Ground pins, and the Trig as well as Echo pins enable it to send and get information with the Arduino. Get familiar with Interfacing Ultrasonic sensor with Arduino here.

The engine shield ought to have at any rate 2 yields, and they ought to be associated with your 2 engines. Regularly, these yields are named "M1" and "M2" or "Engine 1" and "Engine 2". Wire your batteries and power bank up to the engine shield and Arduino separately. Try not to cross interface them. Your engine shield ought to have an information channel. In case you're utilizing wires, associate them to AC connectors.

Programing Explanation:

Open the Arduino IDE. Glue the total Arduino code, given toward the finish of this instructional exercise, into the IDE. Associate your Arduino to the PC. Select the port in Tools/Port. Snap the transfer catch.

Test the robot. In case it turns nearly nothing or to an extreme, explore different avenues regarding the deferrals until impeccable.

Prior to going into the code, we have to introduce the Adafruit Motor Shield Library to drive the DC engines. Since we are utilizing the L293D engine driver shield, we have to download the AFmotor Library from here. At that point include it into your Arduino IDE library organizer. Guarantee you rename it to AFMotor. Become familiar with introducing this library.

Code is simple and can be seen effectively, yet here we have clarified few pieces of it:

Underneath code sets up the robot. First we have incorporated the Adafruit Library for driving the engines with Motor driver shield. From that point forward, we characterized Trig stick and Echo stick. It additionally sets up the engines. It sets the Trig stick to yield and the Echo stick to include.

```
#include <AFMotor.h>

#define trigPin 12

#define echoPin 13

AF_DCMotor motor1(1,MOTOR12_64KHZ);

AF_DCMotor motor2(2, MOTOR12_8KHZ);

void setup() {

  pinMode(trigPin, OUTPUT);

  pinMode(echoPin, INPUT);

}
```

Underneath code advises the Arduino to circle the accompanying directions. From that point onward, it utilizes the sensor to transmit and get ultrasonic sounds. It computes the separation it is from the item once ultrasonic waves ricochets back, in the wake of taking note of that the article is inside the set separation, it advises the Arduino to pivot the engines in like manner.

```
void loop() {

  long duration, distance;

  digitalWrite(trigPin, LOW);

  delayMicroseconds(2);

  digitalWrite(trigPin, HIGH);

  delayMicroseconds(10);

  digitalWrite(trigPin, LOW);

  duration = pulseIn(echoPin, HIGH);

  distance = (duration/2) / 29.1;

  if (distance < 20) {

  motor1.setSpeed(255);

  motor2.setSpeed(0);

  motor1.run(BACKWARD);

  motor2.run(BACKWARD);
```

```
delay(2000); //CHANGE THIS ACCORDING TO
HOW THE ROBOT TURNS.
```

This makes the robot turn by pivoting one engine and keeping the other dormant.

Beneath code makes the robot turn the two engines a similar way so as to make it push ahead until it distinguishes an item in the previously mentioned limit.

```
else {

    motor1.setSpeed(160); //CHANGE THIS AC-
CORDING TO HOW FAST YOUR ROBOT SHOULD
GO.

    motor2.setSpeed(160); //CHANGE THIS TO THE
SAME VALUE AS YOU PUT IN ABOVE.

    motor1.run(FORWARD);

    motor2.run(FORWARD);

}
```

Code

```
#include <AFMotor.h>
#define trigPin 12
#define echoPin 13
```

Anbazhagan K

```
AF_DCMotor motor1(1,MOTOR12_64KHZ);
AF_DCMotor motor2(2, MOTOR12_8KHZ);
void setup() {
  pinMode(trigPin, OUTPUT);
  pinMode(echoPin, INPUT);
}
void loop() {
  long duration, distance;
  digitalWrite(trigPin, LOW);
  delayMicroseconds(2);
  digitalWrite(trigPin, HIGH);
  delayMicroseconds(10);
  digitalWrite(trigPin, LOW);
  duration = pulseIn(echoPin, HIGH);
  distance = (duration/2) / 29.1;
  if(distance < 20) {
motor1.setSpeed(255);
motor2.setSpeed(0);
motor1.run(BACKWARD);
motor2.run(BACKWARD);
delay(2000); //CHANGE THIS ACCORDING TO HOW
THE ROBOT TURNS.
}
  else {
motor1.setSpeed(160); //CHANGE THIS ACCORDING
TO HOW FAST YOUR ROBOT SHOULD GO.
    motor2.setSpeed(160); //CHANGE THIS TO THE
SAME VALUE AS YOU PUT IN ABOVE.
    motor1.run(FORWARD);
    motor2.run(FORWARD);
}
```

}

THANK YOU FOLKS !!!